To a non-Christian,
the Bible is just another book,
to be evaluated as such.
The Christian accepts it on faith, but a faith
well-supported by the internal and external
evidence—evidence which shows
that the Scriptures are inspired by God.

—Roger J. Voskuyl,
President, Westmont College
(Former Chemistry professor, Wheaton College)

CONTENTS

**A teaching and discussion guide for use with this book
is available from your Sunday School Supplier or your
local Christian Bookstore.**

Who Says ?

A discussion of basic questions on the Christian faith, including the existence of God, the trustworthiness of the Bible, the "conflict" between science and Scripture.

EDITOR: Fritz Ridenour

WRITING AND RESEARCH CONSULTANTS
David Harvey (Chapters 1-3)
Georgiana Walker (Chapters 4-7)
Jack Durkee (Chapters 8-12)
David F. Siemens, Jr. (Chapters 8 and 9)

ILLUSTRATOR: Joyce Thimsen

A division of G/L Publications
Glendale, California, U.S.A.

Over 155,000 in print

Second Printing, 1968
Third Printing, 1968
Fourth Printing, 1969
Fifth Printing, 1969
©Copyright 1967 G/L Publications

Printed in U.S.A.

Published by
Regal Books Division, G/L Publications
Glendale, California, U.S.A.

Library of Congress Catalog Card No. 68-16268

Foreword

A study of apologetics—even at a "popular" level—makes you painfully aware of your limitations. We are aware that there is much we have not read and a great deal more that we do not know. We are also aware that in a book of this size there is not enough space to include everything that we would like.

We are also aware that some readers may say we give too much space to the orthodox side and try to "protect the traditional establishment." Others may say we bring up too many arguments that are voiced by the rationalists and believers in scientism.

What we are trying to do, however, is face the situation as we believe it exists. This is an age of astounding scientific advancement. As this book goes to press, the first transplants of human hearts are a reality. Man's landing on the moon is to come shortly. Surely man has reason to be tempted into believing he is his own god and that the "God of the Bible" is adequate for only superstitious and childish minds.

But this is also a day of moral decay, fear of annihilation of the human race by atomic warfare or at best enslavement under a communist bloc that is committed to world domination. Ironically, the communist mind, with its materialistic, atheistic disregard for human dignity, is an end result of rationalistic agnosticism that has been pushed beyond its own built-in moral weaknesses.

Where is man to turn? Who says man has *any place* to turn? The Bible says man can still turn to God. The agnostics, the intellectuals and rationalists, and the evolutionists say man can turn to . . . man.

There is much talk today of man's existential dilemma, of man's hopeless "aloneness" and anxiety. The great battles over inspiration of Scripture, miracles in the Bible, and evolution have supposedly all been fought. Young and old generations are supposedly not asking, "Is the Bible true?" but "Does it make any difference?" Yet, we have the distinct feeling that the "battle of the Bible" is not over and that it never will be. We believe that many people (particularly high school and college ages) have questions about the trustworthiness of the Bible and the divinity of Christ.

Many young people who have "come up through the church" often experience an unpleasant shock when they hit college or the business world or even before they leave high school. The Christian truths and values that they have accepted without question are suddenly challenged and seem to carry no more weight on the open market of ideas than any other viewpoint.

Secular man asks "Just who says the Bible is inspired by God and more authoritative than any other book?" and "Who says that Jesus Christ was really God Himself and therefore in authority over all men?"

While being far from what we would consider the "last word" on these matters, *Who Says?* attempts to help the reader (be he Christian, non-Christian, or undecided) weigh both sides of the question. There is a great deal of evidence for both sides, but there is "no final proof" for either side.

In the final analysis, it is a matter of choice—of faith. There are those who have joined with Julian Huxley to conclude that today God is an "inadequate hypothesis" and man must have faith only in himself.

But there are also many (including scientists and "intellects" of all kinds) who have chosen God. They have said simply, without fanfare, "Lord, *to whom can I go?* You have the words of eternal life."

Fritz Ridenour
Youth Editor, Gospel Light Publications

Just WHO SAYS Christians have 'the answer'?

"*Who says* God is really there? Have you ever seen Him?"

"*Who says* the Bible is so special—infallible, inspired and inerrant? Aren't there all kinds of mistakes in the Bible?"

"*Who says* you can trust the Bible? Wasn't it written by human beings just like us? And many of them were ignorant and uneducated at that . . ."

"*Who says* fulfilled prophecy is any proof for the Bible's inspiration? A few lucky guesses, a coincidence or two—that doesn't mean much."

"*Who says* archaeology helps prove the Bible is true? Since when can you dig up proof to substantiate *myths*?"

"*Who says* evolution isn't the real answer to where life came from? Why it's the only possible natural explanation. Man evolved with the apes—from a common primate ancestor."

"*Who says* Genesis I is believable to any educated

person in this scientific age? Six days to make the earth? Ridiculous!"

"*Who says* science isn't making tremendous progress? Space travel is already here. Disease is practically conquered. Man will soon control birth, life, death—even control the brain and program it any way he likes."

"*Who says* that the church and the Bible — that religions of any kind—are even relevant to modern man? Science has gone farther in the last 50 years than Christianity has gone in 2000. Religion is obsolete!"

Questions like the above are what this book is all about. The question is asked quite often these days—"Who says?" Who says anything is right or wrong? Good or evil? True or false? And who says that Christianity—with that special book called the Bible—has any corner on wisdom or authority? Who says *anyone* has any authority to tell someone else how to live?

This book is built on one basic answer to the basic question, "Who says?"

God says . . .

Not "Christianity". . . not "the church". . . not "religion". . . but God . . . *the God of the Bible.*

The Bible makes it clear—from cover to cover—that it is *God* who says that He is the Creator of the universe and the One who keeps it going. It is God who created all living things. It is God who created man in His own image. It is God who tells man what he needs to know. It is God who gives man direction and purpose for his life.

But there is an obvious question. Just who says that we can be sure that the Bible is really God's message to men? Who says the Bible is truly a unique book? Who says the Bible isn't merely a record of how the Jews (and then later a sect of fanatic followers of Jesus) developed their own peculiar ideas about religion?

2

QUESTIONS LIKE THESE ARE WHAT THIS BOOK IS ALL ABOUT

Questions that challenge the authority and trustworthiness of the Bible are the basis for a special system of study called "Christian apologetics." This doesn't mean that Christians "apologize" for their faith. Nor does it mean that Christians make embarrassed excuses for their Bible, which contains "awkward" statements such as "All have sinned..." and strange tales about men rising from the dead and floating around in fish.

Instead, apologetics is a rational defense of Christian-

APOLOGETICS DOESN'T MEAN MAKING EXCUSES
FOR YOUR FAITH . . .

ity and the divine origin of the Bible. Convinced
Christians may say with fervor that the Bible and their
faith need no defense—that God has spoken and "that's
it." While this may be true for the convinced Christian,
it misses the point. These are days when all authority is
being questioned. Christianity is being rejected because
too many Christians are ignorant of how their faith and
their Bible relate to the world and reality. Too many
Christians are unable to voice their beliefs in a rational,
meaningful way. The result is that many people reject
a caricature of true Christianity, because they have mistaken ideas about what the gospel really means. These
mistaken ideas often arise because all that people hear
from Christians is, "God said it in the Bible, and that's
it." But that isn't "it" for a lot of people (and they are
not all necessarily outside of the church).

Many Christians are quizzed frequently about their
beliefs by friends, classmates and associates. Sometimes
the quizzing is open ridicule; sometimes it takes the
form of subtle innuendos; and Christians are also sub-
tly tested by those who seem to ignore Christianity.
Sometimes, however, Christians are asked about their
faith by sincere seekers after spiritual truth.

If you are a typical Christian, you are probably a
prime candidate for the school of Christian apologetics.

Chances are you have been looking for some specific, practical help for defending and explaining what you believe . . . something that gets down to the nitty-gritty . . . the world you must live in at least six days of the week . . . the world where "Have faith, brother" isn't the panacea for all problems.

Not that "having faith" isn't important. Faith is the spiritual life's blood of the Christian. "You can never please God without faith, without depending on Him" (Heb. 11:6 *Living Letters*). Many Christians long for some reasons, some explanations, some sensible answers for questions that are directed at them and their Bible by a rationalistic, unbelieving, secular, scientific world. To want reasonable answers is no disgrace, nor is it some sort of sinful slide "to the rear of the spiritual bus."

The Christian faith rests on facts—the central fact being the life, death and resurrection of Jesus Christ. Christians are urged to have "a reasonable answer," to be ready to tell others why they believe as they do. (See I Peter 3:15, *Living Letters*.) And Isaiah says "Come now, and let us reason together . . ." (Isa. 1:18).

And so this book accepts the formidable task of dealing with typical questions about the Bible, Christ and the Christian faith. Although written primarily to

NOR IS APOLOGETICS AN ALL OUT ATTACK ON UNBELIEVERS.

TO WANT REASONABLE ANSWERS IS NOT SOME KIND OF SINFUL SLIDE TO THE REAR OF THE SPIRITUAL BUS . . .

help committed Christians, *Who Says?* may be helpful to the non-Christian or the "turned-off" Christian as well. *Who Says?* will not be a "proof text party." Scripture will be cited, to be sure, but only with the purpose of explaining what the Bible says about a certain question and why.

Make no mistake . . . *what the Bible says* is the central issue.

The Bible is revelation—God revealing Himself to man, disclosing His will and His plan for the world. The Bible brings man the gospel—"the good news" about how God has acted in history to communicate to man, to save him for Himself, to help him out of the fatal dilemma called sin.

Again and again the Christian comes back to the importance of Scripture. If Scripture is true, the Christian has a case. If Scripture is false, the Christian has a quaint religion that is equal to folklore. Is there solid evidence for the truth and credibility of the Bible? *Definitely* . . . and this book presents the evidence by meeting the common questions and criticisms concerning the Bible and Christianity head on. Atheism, agnosticism, "higher criticism" of the Bible, evolutionism, scientism ... all of these are dealt with. The Bible has nothing to hide, but, as the evidence points out, perhaps some of the critics do. The skeleton in many a critic's closet is his bias against the supernatural. If a person prefers to believe that the supernatural is impossible and that the only real truth is the truth found in test tubes, mathematical equations and the reasoning of man, then he will find the Bible a baffling book indeed. However, as even many of the most agnostically inclined thinkers are beginning to realize, all truth is not contained in logarithms or human logic. Man is a spiritual as well as a rational being and in the final analysis a man finds his idea of truth where he is willing to put his faith and trust.

No one should keep this more clearly in mind than the Christian. Although the Christian can offer many pieces of evidence for the Truth of the Bible, he must always be aware that Christianity cannot be "proved" with formulas or overwhelming collections of facts.

THE SKELETON IN MANY A BIBLE CRITIC'S CLOSET IS A BASIC BIAS AGAINST THE SUPERNATURAL. . .

Every person who is confronted with the Truth in the Bible and Christ must weigh the evidence for himself and then decide if he will place his faith in what he finds or if he will reject it and seek "truth" somewhere else. The writer of Hebrews has stated the issue clearly: "Anyone who wants to come to God must believe that there is a God and that He will reveal Himself to those who sincerely look for him" (Heb. 11:6, *Living Letters*).

CHAPTER 1

How can you know there is a God?

A rather basic question—perhaps almost "too elementary" for some people—concerns the very existence of God Himself. Yet, even the most convinced believer has his moments of doubt, those times when (if he's honest with himself) he wonders if "God is really there."

During today's scientific technological explosion, there are many people who claim that God is simply a superstitious idea that man is finally outgrowing. The 1960's saw the rise of a radical group of religious thinkers who decreed the paradoxical slogan, "God is dead!" But the "God is dead" idea is nothing new. Back in the 1850's, Friedrich Nietzsche, a German philosopher, coined the phrase "God is dead" as he developed an anti-Christian system of thought that included the concept of a "master race," foundation for the ideas of twentieth century madman Adolph Hitler.

It is nothing new that man doubts the existence of

God ... or is it more accurate to say that he wishes God weren't there? Throughout history, man has been incurably God-conscious, whether seeking God or trying to deny that He even exists. Could it be that Augustine was right? "Thou hast made us for Thyself, O God, and our hearts are restless until they rest in Thee."

What do people mean when they use the word "God"?

Some concepts of God have been quite small. For example, since the dawn of history many men have searched for a god that will give them comfort and security, but who will not require much of them. Many men have been content with a god that will make their crops grow, keep them safe from their enemies, and who will provide a place for their souls after death, but along with all this they want a god who will allow them to have "a little fun" (sin a little) once in a while.

You can still find this approach to God today, among pagan savages and even among people living right next door. In *Your God Is Too Small*, J. B. Phillips describes many of the "unreal gods" that people still believe in today. One of these is the "grand old man," the fatherly white-haired God in heaven who smiles down on men and overlooks their "little mistakes" such as adultery, cheating, stealing, selfishness, cruelty, slander, etc., ad infinitum. The popular idea that goes along with this kind of God is that ". . . as long as I'm good, mind my own business and never kill anyone the grand old man in the sky will be pleased with me."*

*See Your God Is Too Small, J. B. Phillips, the Macmillan Company, Macmillan Paperbacks Edition 1961, p. 23. Other Gods discussed by Phillips in this provocative little book include: "The Resident Policeman, (Man's Conscience); "Parental Hangover": "Gentle Jesus Meek and Mild": "Absolute Perfection" (The God of One Hundred Percent); "The God in a Box" (The God that fits certain sectarian and denominational ideas); "The Managing Director" (The God of the deist who is too big and too far away to ever be involved with individuals).

THE "GRAND OLD MAN" KIND OF GOD OVERLOOKS OUR LITTLE "MISTAKES" LIKE SELFISHNESS, CRUELTY, FORNICATION, ETC., ETC.

Men are quite content with the "grand old man" or some other man-made idea of God with which they are comfortable. But the view of God that makes them uncomfortable (if not angry) is in the Bible. The chief objection many people have to such a God is that He is not man-made. On the contrary, it is God who made man (Gen. 1:1, Psalm 100:3) and who has power, wisdom and knowledge far beyond human capabilities.

The God of the Bible makes many people nervous. They are no longer in control of the situation. This kind of God is a bit too big for comfort. The God of the Bible requires everything of man. He requires man to confess that he is a sinner and that he is in need of help that only God can give him. At the base of man's sin is pride that will not let him admit that he needs this help. Is it really so surprising that proud sinful man says that the message from the God of the Bible is "no longer meaningful" today? He doesn't want it to be!

What basic attitudes do people hold toward God today?

If you were to take a "man on the street" poll you would find several basic concepts of God.

The atheist says that there is no God. He rules out all

11

ideas of God, from the views of the savage to those of the Christian. The atheist would say that the gods of the Greeks and the God of the Bible are all the same—myths and fables that no educated, scientifically minded person could possibly believe in.

Many atheists are so emotional about their views that it seems atheism is some sort of religion in its own right. Some atheists go to any end to remove references to God from public institutions. Some are very much opposed to organized religion. For example, Madelyn Murray gained national prominence in the United States in 1962 when she instituted court proceedings that resulted in a supreme court ruling against the reading of the Bible in public schools.*

Although people like Madelyn Murray often gain a great deal of publicity, hard core atheists are in the minority. Much more common is . . .

The agnostic holds that neither the existence of God nor the origin of the universe is known or knowable. The agnostic does not simply say "I do not know if there is a God." He makes the universal negative judgment that, "I *cannot* know if there is a God."

Ironically, a universal negative judgment of this kind requires some kind of universal knowledge in order to be true.** In other words, how does the agnostic know that he cannot know? The agnostic simply substitutes one absolute (God and His truths) for another absolute (his own opinions that he cannot possibly know God).

The deist moves beyond the agnostic to believe that

---

*See "War on God," **Saturday Evening Post,** July, 1964.
Criticisms of agnosticism also apply to atheism. As J. Edwin Orr points out in **100 Questions About God, Regal Books, 1966, p. 40, in order to be an atheist you'd need to know everything, otherwise you could never be sure that there wasn't a God. In other words, an atheist is faced with the question, "Couldn't God exist outside the fraction of your personal knowledge of all that there is to know?"

there is a God but only in a "limited sort of way." Deists believe that God created the universe and set it up to run perfectly and precisely like a well-oiled machine or clock. After God got everything running properly, however, He turned His back on His creation and had no more to do with it. Therefore, the deist believes that man cannot communicate with God.

Deism was popular in England and America in the 17th and 18th centuries. Many famous men such as Sir Isaac Newton, Benjamin Franklin and Thomas Jefferson were deists.

The theist is the person who accepts the idea of one God. Jews, Moslems and Christians are all theists. In America the typical man on the street considers himself a theist "who believes the Bible." Many such people, of course, have read little or none of the Bible and have no idea of what they mean specifically by saying they believe in God. But they are like the little boy who wrote a short but to-the-point letter: "Dear God, please count me in."*

The Christian not only believes that there is a God, but that God visited this planet in human form. Jesus Christ lived a perfect and sinless life, then died as a sacrifice for man's sins and rose from the dead to guarantee eternal life to all who believe in Him.

Apart from the Bible, what are "proofs" for the existence of God?

Over the years men have argued about the existence of God by using several basic approaches:

The cosmological argument insists that the cosmos (world) must have an explanation. This argument says that the world could not simply have "just happened."

---

*Children's Letters to God, compiled by Eric Marshall and Stuart Hample. Copyright 1966, Marshall and Hample. Simon & Schuster, Inc., p. 1.

There must be a cause equal to its effect. Paul used the cosmological argument when he wrote: "Since earliest times men have seen the earth and sky and all God made, and have known of His existence and great eternal power" (Rom. 1:20, *Living Letters*).

The teleological argument is closely associated with the cosmological approach. Teleology means that the design of the universe implies that there was purpose or direction behind it and that someone must have designed it.

Psalm 19:1 speaks of how design points to a Designer: "The heavens declare the glory of God and the firmament showeth His handiwork."

The rational argument points out that the world operates according to order and natural law and therefore there must be a mind behind this order and law.

There are people, however, who reject cosmological, teleological or rational arguments for God's existence. These people prefer to believe that the world is a product of "natural forces" working more or less by chance. The earth, living things, man himself . . . all are results of a "lucky cosmic accident."

Scientist A. Cressy Morrison points to some interesting possibilities if the design of the universe were altered only slightly. For example, the earth now rotates on its axis in 24 hours at the rate of about 1,000 miles an hour. Why couldn't it rotate at the rate of 100 miles an hour? If it did, the earth's days and nights would be ten times longer than they are now, with the result that the hot summer sun would burn vegetation and the long cold nights would freeze it. Do you see the point? It is no accident that our "days" are 24 hours long.

There are countless other facts that are difficult to explain "by chance." Even the position of the moon— 240,000 miles away—is significant. If the moon were

14

THERE ARE SEVERAL STANDARD ARGUMENTS
TO "PROVE" GOD EXISTS . . .

only 50,000 miles away, the tides of the ocean would be so huge that eventually all the mountains on various continents would be eroded away and there would be daily hurricanes.*

The ontological argument follows the idea that man can conceive of the idea of perfection—of God. Where does man get his idea of God, but from God Himself?

Studies by anthropologists show that man is incurably God-conscious. This God-consciousness has often been corrupted and warped by polytheism and idolatry, but the desire to know God is still there. The Christian believes this desire is evidence for God. If God were

*See *Man Does Not Stand Alone*, A. Cressy Morrison. Copyright 1944, Fleming H. Revell Company. Chapter 1, "Our Unique World," pp. 13-19.

not real and He had not placed in man a desire to know Him, man would have no need to seek God. In addition man would have no need to go to such great effort to deny Him as atheists and agnostics do. In other words, if man did not have any real reason or cause within himself to believe that God exists, man would make no fuss about it. He would think about God about as often as a caterpillar would recite the Gettysburg address.

The moral argument holds that man has a built-in sense of right and wrong that cannot be accounted for except by looking to the Someone who created man and gave him this sense in the first place.

In *Mere Christianity,* C. S. Lewis observes that people get into quarrels by appealing to some kind of standard of behavior they expect the other person to know about. Whether the quarrel is major, ("you stole my wife") or whether it is minor ("you can't sit here; I'm saving these seats"), one party is always trying to show the other party where they are in the wrong and as Lewis points out, there is no sense in trying to do this unless both parties are appealing to some sort of basic agreement as to what is right and wrong in the first place. The question is, where did they get this sense of right and wrong?*

Can any argument "prove" that God exists?

Many Christians make the mistake of thinking they can take evidences for the existence of God and argue people into the Kingdom. For example, the Christian does see evidence for the existence of God in the orderliness of the universe. The design of the universe truly points to a designer. Those who press the teleological and rational arguments point to the precision of the workings of the universe, the predictability of the

*See **Mere Christianity,** C. S. Lewis, Macmillan paperbacks, 1960, pp. 15-19.

rising and setting of the sun, the ebb and the flow of the tides. A real "clincher" for this argument is the point that science would be impossible in a world which was not created by a rational orderly God, who caused things to operate the same way day after day and century after century.

If you wish to do so, you can conclude that the orderliness and design of the universe make this the "best of all possible worlds" as did Dr. Pangloss, the naive philosopher in the book, *Candide*, written by the master satirist and anti-Biblical agnostic, Voltaire (Francois Marie Arouet). Voltaire wrote *Candide* in 1759 as a direct attack on the teleological argument that for every effect, there is a cause and that the orderliness of the universe proves that it was created by a loving and perfect God.

With ruthless precision and sensual sarcasm, Voltaire has the characters in *Candide* (including the hero, who is Candide himself) going through all kinds of horrors and calamities that show that this world also contains a great deal of disorder and chaos. Fornication, adultery, rape, murder, the carnage of war, and the chaos of earthquakes killing thousands are all described with gusto by Voltaire in his brief, but potent little story of *Candide*.

Voltaire's point in writing the book is to ask how violent death, war, famine, earthquake, disease, etc., can exist in an "orderly world" that is created by an orderly God who cares for His creation. Voltaire is asking a basic question that many people still ask today . . .

If God made the world and controls it, why is there evil?

The stock reply is that evil came into the world because of man's sin. There are many proof texts to back up this idea, but many people (including many Christians) are still puzzled by the quandary that is posed when someone asks: "If God is a God of love and He is all-powerful and all-wise, how can He possibly allow so much suffering in His creation and among those He has created?" In other words, it seems to a lot of people that the existence of evil "proves" that God really isn't all-loving or all-powerful because if He were, He would somehow get rid of evil and make this world a completely "happy" place in which to live.

There are no easy or complete answers to the dilemma posed by these questions. No one knows (or will ever know exactly) how allowing the existence of evil can be part of God's plan, and, as C. S. Lewis has pointed out, it is easier to talk about pain than to experience it.* There are, however, several basic considerations that can help the Christian grapple with this problem and see some of the fallacies in reasoning that because evil exists, God cannot be all-powerful or all-good.

One way to break the question down is to examine evil in two parts: 1) "natural evil" (tragedy occurring in natural events); 2) "moral evil" (evil done by man). Actually, moral evil done by sinful man is easier to understand than is "natural" evil. Natural evil includes such calamities as tornado and earthquake, fire and flood, the birth of deformed children, disease, etc. Why does God let these things happen? And more precisely, everyone asks, "Why does He let things like this happen to *me?*"

J. B. Phillips observes that we are mistaken if we think that life on this planet can be automatically safe.** C. S. Lewis points out that God made men free

*See **The Problem of Pain**, C. S. Lewis, Macmillan paperbacks edition, 1963, p. 105.
See **God Our Contemporary, J. B. Phillips, Macmillan paperbacks edition, 1960, p. 92.

with the alternative of choice, and God also made nature, which He set up according to rational, dependable laws that work the same way every time. Natural laws cause earthquakes, floods, tornadoes, etc. Natural law also causes fire to be comfortably warm at one distance, but fire can also burn if you get too close. To ask God to change natural law for the convenience of one person or group of persons at a certain time or place would be to ask God to equally inconvenience other people in other situations at the same time. Lewis believes that God does not change the world at every man's whim and for every man's convenience. God may choose to control matter and overrule the laws of nature, and when He does so, we call it a miracle. The very concept, however, of a common, stable world rules out the idea of miracles happening frequently. Lewis concludes that if you try to exclude the possibilities of suffering (the "risks" of living), which are inevitable when free wills exist in the order of nature, you would have to rule out life itself.[*]

Man's free will, his option of choice, is also an integral part of the reason for "moral evil"—the result of "man's inhumanity to man." According to C. S. Lewis, human wickedness (a result of the fall of man into sin) accounts for perhaps four-fifths of the suffering endured by men.[**] Our immediate reply to this is "Why doesn't God stop evil men from making others suffer?" J. B. Phillips asks, however, how would God intervene and not interfere with the gift of personal choice (free will)?[***] And, there is also the question, "Just how much evil do you want God to stop?" If God were to

[*] See **The Problem of Pain**, pp. 26-34. Lewis also points out that God does not do the intrinsically impossible (something that is self-contradictory). God created the natural world for us to live in. He also gave us free will. If God were to control the natural world in order to "save us from our mistakes," He would contradict the principle of free will.
[**] See **The Problem of Pain**, p. 89.
[***] See **God Our Contemporary**, p. 89.

start judging every person with perfect justice, who would stand until nightfall?*

Another aspect of evil that bothers many people is the apparent "unfairness of it all." Often it seems that the innocent suffer and the wicked get away with it. But as J. B. Phillips points out, there is obsolutely no teaching anywhere in the Bible that when a man tries to please God he is guaranteed complete protection from evil by divine intervention. Christ's own life on earth refutes this idea.**

What the Bible does promise is that nothing can separate us from the love of God (Romans 8:39) and that God's resources for facing trouble are always available to us, no matter what may come (Romans 5:1-11).

It is difficult to grapple with the question of evil and suffering. It is infinitely more difficult to experience evil and suffering in its many forms, be it disease, accident, natural disaster or cruel treatment. It may help, however, to remember:

1. God does not do the intrinsically impossible; therefore He does not put men with free wills into a world that operates by natural law without the frequent result of what we call "pain" or "suffering."

2. The possession of free will and the power of choice in man is the "risk that God had to take," knowing full well that evil could result if man made the wrong choice.

Exactly why God gave man this choice is often hard to understand when one sees "all the evil" that has come from it. But then we face another question: "Would not the denial of this choice have been an even greater evil still?"

*See "What Non-Christians Ask," Paul E. Little, His magazine reprint.
**See God Our Contemporary, pp. 89-92. See also the most profound explanation for suffering in Scripture, the Book of Job.

What if my friends tell me that putting faith in God is just a crutch?

Non-Christians often charge a believer with the claims that "God is just a crutch," which Christians use to keep from facing reality and responsibility for their own actions and destiny. This kind of criticism makes the Christian sound like he is some sort of weak-kneed, spineless jellyfish, who is afraid to face life as it really is. But the charge that "God is a crutch" misses the point. If God has created the world and everything in it, including man himself, it follows that man owes God his worship and obedience. It is difficult to see how a man could call his Maker a crutch.

The Christian is only acknowledging what he finds in the revelation of God—the Scriptures—which tell him that he owes his very existence to God (Acts 17:28). Instead of a "crutch" it would be more accurate to say that God is the believer's "iron lung." Ironically enough, God is the unbeliever's "iron lung" as well and when the unbeliever refuses to acknowledge that God is the giver of the very air he breathes, he really invents his own particular kind of crutch with which he hopes to hobble away somewhere and hide from God.

If you can't "prove" God exists, how can you know He is there?

In the Bible, there are no arguments to prove God's

existence. There is no attempt to prove God from design, orderliness, a moral sense of right or wrong in man, or through any other argument. Scripture takes God's existence for granted.

Instead of "proving" God exists, the reader of Scripture is invited to trust God and by doing so to prove His reality. In short, the Bible tells man that faith (personal commitment and trust) is the only real "proof" of God.

The writer of Hebrews tells us that faith "is the confident assurance that something we want is going to happen. It is the certainty that what we hope for is waiting for us, even though we cannot see it up ahead" (Hebrews 11:1, *Living Letters*).

You cannot prove God by laboratory experiment. Nor can you prove God by logical and rational arguments. If God were the last step in a clever, philosophical argument, then the most intelligent and well-trained people would be the first to believe. And, those who could not follow an involved argument or chain of reasoning would have little chance to know God. God has chosen, however, to offer certainty about Himself on an entirely different basis. *It is the person who believes who knows*, not the one who is most clever with logic or ideas. It is the person who trusts in God, even though he cannot see Him or measure Him, who really has assurance that there is a God and that he has a personal relationship with God. (See Heb. 11:6.)

The point is this: You can follow all the arguments people may give you for the existence of God, but for every argument *for* the existence of God, you can find someone who will offer an argument *against* it. Eventually, you have to take a "leap of faith" and put your trust in God. You have to take God at His word—which you find in the Bible.

How can you take the "leap of faith"?

One way to think about the "leap of faith" is to consider a sport that has grown very popular in recent years: skydiving. Imagine leaping out of an airplane at some 5,000 feet and then falling through space at 120 miles an hour until you are quite close to the ground before pulling the rip cord.

Skydivers will tell you that they're rather nervous on their first jump—that is, their first dive through space. As one skydiver has said: "You just gotta have faith in that chute, that it'll open up when it's supposed to. Then you find out it does. It works and you don't even bother to think about that part of it again. It's just that first time. Sooner or later you just gotta step out . . . in faith."*

Actually skydivers operate with three elements that are similar to the three-part definition of faith given by Charles Spurgeon, one of the greatest preachers in history. Spurgeon believed that faith is made up of knowledge, belief and trust.

Knowledge comes first. You have to be informed of a fact before you can possibly believe it. The skydiver can "know" that this sport is exciting, but still relatively safe, through observation, reading and talking to other people. In just the same way, the Christian who observes the world around him, who reads the Scriptures and who talks to others who have experienced God, can know that there is a God—a God who, in Jesus Christ, actually broke into the stream of history to do something for man.

From knowledge (mental assent) a person must go on to belief. The skydiving candidate must "believe" what

*Adapted from Study Guide for the Gospel Light Publications 12th grade Bible Study course, What's Your Answer? Vol. I.

**SOONER OR LATER
YOU JUST GOTTA STEP OUT IN FAITH**

he sees and reads and hears. He must say to himself, "Yes, now I have the facts and I accept them. I believe that skydiving is a perfectly safe sport and that the chute will open, because of the evidence." In exactly the same way, the person who is seeking God says the same thing: "Yes, I believe that God does exist because I've seen the world He made, I've read about Him in His Book and I have talked to others who have experienced Him as well."

The third and vital step, however, is trust. The skydiver knows in a real sense what it means to trust, to just "step out in faith."

As Spurgeon pointed out, trust is the element that makes the real difference ... to trust Christ and turn yourself completely over to Him and admit you have no other alternative. Spurgeon observed that it was one thing to understand the gospel and what you should do and it is another thing to do it. He preferred to see the poorest kind of real faith rather than the finest kind of "understanding" of what the Bible teaches but no real trust in Christ. Knowledge of God is one thing, but there must be follow-through. There must be trust—complete reliance on the Lord Jesus Christ—in order to be saved.*

*Spurgeon's thoughts on faith adapted from "What Is Faith?", one in a volume of his sermons which is entitled **All of Grace**, Moody Press.

For further reading

Paperbacks

Mere Christianity, C. S. Lewis, Macmillan Paperbacks, 1960. See especially Book I (Right and Wrong as a Clue to the Meaning of the Universe) and Book II (What Christians Believe). Some of Lewis' best apologetic arguments are found here.

The Problem of Pain, C. S. Lewis, Macmillan Paperbacks, 1962. The entire book is excellent, and chapters 2 ("Divine Omnipotence") 3 ("Divine Goodness") 4 ("Human Wickedness") and 5 ("The Fall of Man") are especially useful concerning the question of evil.

Candide, Voltaire (Francois Marie Arouet), translated by Lowell Bair, Bantam Books, 1959. A graphic example of how an unbelieving agnostic can tear down the cause and effect argument for the existence of God.

100 Questions About God, J. Edwin Orr, Regal Books, 1966. Chapters 1-8 are useful, particularly in shedding light on the agnostic and the atheistic point of view.

Your God Is Too Small, J. B. Phillips, Macmillan Paperbacks, 1961. See especially the discussion of "unreal gods" in Part I, pp. 15-62.

God Our Contemporary, J. B. Phillips, Macmillan Paperbacks, 1960. See especially Chapters 14 and 15 ("Some Criticisms of Christianity") and Chapters 16 and 17 ("Problems of Suffering and Evil").

Hardbacks

An Introduction to Christian Apologetics, Edward J. Carnell, Eerdman's, 1948. Chapters 7-10 of this work on apologetics deal with the knowledge of God that comes from nature, man himself, and special revelation.

Out of the Depths, Helmut Thielicke, Wm. B. Eerdmans, 1962. See especially Chapter 1 ("The God of Ends"). This chapter helps the Christian understand how he can face tragedy.

The Universe: Plan or Accident? Robert E. D. Clark, Muhlenberg Press, 1961. See especially Chapter 16 ("Evil").

CHAPTER 2

If there is a God,
how can I know Him?

Many people will admit there is a "God of some kind" or perhaps a "force of some kind" behind the universe, but they are completely in the dark about how to know this God in a real and personal way. A lot of people may claim that they believe God exists, but as far as their daily lives are concerned, God is far away and seemingly uninvolved.

It appears that there is a "communications gap" between God and man. The following questions and answers go into the nature of this "communications gap" and how God has bridged the gap and revealed Himself to man. The Bible plainly teaches that man can know God *if he wants to.*

Why is there a "gap" between God and man?

Some people would blame God for the so-called gap between Him and humanity. Typical remarks include, "If there is a God, why can't I see Him?" or "Why doesn't God prove He's really there? Why doesn't He do something or say something?"

Atheists are well-known for inviting God to strike them dead. Even the Jews, devout believers in God, show a history of wanting Him to "show them a sign" to assure them that He is concerned about communicating with them.

Scripture, however, points out that God is always taking the initative to communicate with man and that the reason for the "communications gap" is man's sin, not God's "neglect." God created man to love Him and in order to love someone you have to communicate with him. But man chose to go his own way. He disobeyed God and took advantage of the freedom that God gave him. Man himself created the "communications gap" between himself and God and man is powerless to bridge that gap alone.

Has God bridged the gap?

If man can't bridge the gap, then it is up to God. Has He any "bridges" that can help man get in touch with Him? There are at least three:

God reveals Himself in nature. As chapter 1 pointed out, "The heavens declare the glory of God ..." (Ps. 19:1) and "Since earliest times, men have seen the earth and sky and all God made and have known of His existence and great eternal power" (Rom. 1:20, *Living Letters*). Even pagan savages are aware of God by what they see in nature. The cultured Greeks to whom Paul spoke on Mars Hill in Athens were equally aware of "something" or "someone" that was above and beyond

NATURE TAKES YOU PART OF THE WAY . . .

their polytheistic stable of man-made gods. They called this something the "unknown god" and Paul was quick to identify this "unknown god" as the God who made the world and everything in it, but He does not dwell in temples made with hands. (See Acts 17:22-28.)

Natural revelation is a kind of "foot bridge" by which you can span the gap between yourself and God. (Also see Psa. 19:1; 97:6; Acts 14:17.) But there is a better, more substantial bridge—God's written revelation—the Bible.

God reveals Himself through His written and spoken Word. God did not depend on nature alone to reveal Himself to man. He inspired His everlasting Word, the Bible, so that man can know His plans and His directions for living. (See II Peter 1:21; II Tim. 3:16,17.) It is through the Scripture that you can become "personally acquainted" with God and learn His will for your life and His wisdom for all mankind. (See Psa. 19:8; 119:105; Rom. 15:4.)

How can you be sure that the Bible is God's Word and not simply the words of men? This will be discussed in detail in Chapter 3, but for right now keep in mind that we are looking for ways to bridge the gap between God and man. The Bible—if you are willing to believe it is true—is a far more substantial and detailed bridge to God than nature.

God, then, has written a "world book" (nature) and a "word book" (the Bible) to reveal Himself to man, but God has gone even farther than that. God has come to earth and become a man Himself!

The climax of revelation is the incarnation—the appearance of Jesus Christ. In Jesus Christ, God visited this planet (John 1:14). Christ not only taught men how to live; He gave men eternal life through His death and resurrection. Jesus Christ is the main bridge to God. In Christ God completely closes the gap between Himself and man.

Was Jesus God or only a man?

The answer to this question is crucial if you want to have a personal and complete knowledge of God. From the first century until now, people have been trying to claim or prove that Jesus of Nazareth was merely a human teacher, or, at best, something less than God Himself.

THE BIBLE TAKES YOU STILL FARTHER . . .

JESUS CHRIST TAKES YOU ALL THE WAY.

One of the first groups to attack the concept that Jesus is God Himself were the Gnostics, pseudo intellectuals of the first and second centuries who mixed Christianity with pagan philosophy. Among the Gnostic teachings were such ideas as the eternity of matter and that all matter is imperfect and contains the seeds of corruption and evil.

Gnostics taught that there was a difference between the Demi-Urge (the God of the Old Testament) and the God of the New Testament who was the Father of Jesus Christ. Gnostics also taught that Jesus the man was controlled by a "heavenly Christ" who returned to heaven before Jesus was crucified. In effect, the Gnostics reduced Christ to mere humanity. Christ, said the Gnostics, was a man who was deeply influenced by God and who had deep spiritual insights, but He was still only a man.

What do Biblical writers say about Jesus?

Remembering that the testimony of a witness is considered direct evidence in a court of law, consider the words of two of the major contributors to the New

Testament: the apostle John and the apostle Paul.

John opened his Gospel by saying: "In the beginning was the Word, and the Word was with God, and the Word was God. The same was in the beginning with God. All things were made by him; and without him was not any thing made that was made" (John 1:1-3).

John chose the term, "Word" carefully. He wanted to communicate to Greek speaking people as well as Jews. The Jews would understand "Word" because it had Old Testament roots and suggested the concept of the all-powerful word of God.

In Greek (the language John used to write his Gospel) Word means Logos. For those trained in Greek ways of thinking Logos meant "reason"—the mind of God guiding and directing the universe.

In these opening verses, John is saying that the "Word" has always existed and that all things were made by the "Word," but just whom is he talking about? You can jump down to verse 14 to get your answer. "The Word became flesh, and dwelt among us." John is clearly saying that the Word is Jesus Christ and that Christ is God Himself.

John makes a similar reference in his first Epistle where he writes, "That which was from the beginning, which we have heard, which we have seen with our eyes, which we have looked upon, and our hands have handled, of the Word (Logos) of life" (I John 1:1).

John had known Jesus in person and had, in fact, been referred to by Jesus as "His beloved disciple." John had walked and talked with Jesus. He had eaten with Him and listened to His teachings and he was present at the crucifixion as well as on different occasions when Christ appeared after the resurrection. The apostle John knew Jesus Christ to be the perfect expression of God. John knew that in Jesus Christ was all that God wanted man to know about Himself.

Paul knew this as well. While Paul did not walk and talk with Jesus, he did meet Him in a miraculous way on the road to Damascus. From Paul's pen came some of the most profound of Christian Scripture. It is Paul who laid the groundwork for Christian theology in his Epistles to various Christian churches. Paul was, in a special way, just as much an apostle as John was (II Cor. 11:5).

What does Paul say about Jesus? Like John, Paul believed that Jesus Christ was Creator of the universe and that ". . . all things were created by him . . ." (Col. 1:16). Paul also wrote that in Christ dwelt ". . . all the fullness of the Godhead bodily" (Col. 2:9). In I Tim. 3:16 Paul wrote that "God was manifest in the flesh . . ." (meaning Jesus). And, in regard to the communication gap between God and man, Paul said "For there is one God, and one mediator between God and men, the man Christ Jesus" (I Tim. 2:5).

For John, the disciple best loved by Jesus, and for Paul, Christianity's first and greatest missionary and theologian, Jesus Christ and God were one in the same. Their writings stand as clear evidence that Christ was far more than only a good man or an exceptional teacher. He was (and is) God Himself.

Who did Jesus say He was?

There are many theologians and Bible teachers today who claim that Jesus was simply a human being who had a knack for teaching by telling stories and who leaned toward political rebellion.

Did Jesus actually see Himself as divine or was all of this added to the Christian faith by overzealous disciples who got carried away with religious fervor and fantasy? To answer the question, you have to go to the words of Jesus Himself as are recorded in the Gospels. In John 10:30, Jesus plainly stated that "I and my Father are one." In John 14:9, Jesus answered Philip's request to "show us the Father" by telling Philip, "he that hath seen me hath seen the Father."

Jesus also claimed the power to "forgive sins," something that the Jews of His day well realized that only God could do. When He cured a palsied man, Jesus said, "Son, thy sins be forgiven thee." And certain scribes who were watching wondered, "Who can forgive sins but God only?" (See Mark 2:5-11.)

Beyond any doubt Jesus knew and believed that He was God Himself and that He had come to earth for a definite purpose: to "buy men back" for the kingdom of God and to give them life eternal. In Luke 19:10, Jesus said that He had "... come to seek and to save that which was lost," meaning mankind.

When Jesus told the Jews, "Before Abraham was, I am," the significance of His words was not lost upon them. They knew that He was claiming that He was from eternity, that He had lived even before the time of Abraham, 2000 years before.

In the mouth of anyone but God, statements like those above could only be described as pure lunacy. Yet, as you read the Gospels, you hardly get the idea that Jesus was a lunatic. On the contrary, you are aware that you are in the presence of perfect humility, perfect meekness and perfect wisdom.

As C. S. Lewis has pointed out, Jesus was and is the Son of God (and that means God Himself, not a "son" of God by creation in the sense that all men are sons of God), or He is a lunatic. Make one of two choices about Jesus Christ: Laugh at Him, spit at Him, even call Him the devil himself; or fall at His feet and call Him your Lord and your God. But don't go to Jesus with any "patronizing nonsense about His being a great human teacher." The Scripture makes it perfectly plain that that is one option Jesus Christ never left open to us.*

*See Mere Christianity, C. S. Lewis, Copyright 1952, Macmillan, pp. 51-53.

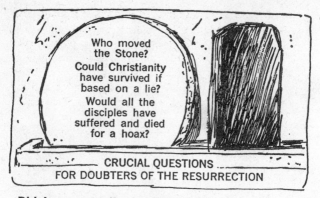

Who moved
the Stone?

Could Christianity
have survived if
based on a lie?

Would all the
disciples have
suffered and died
for a hoax?

CRUCIAL QUESTIONS
FOR DOUBTERS OF THE RESURRECTION

Did Jesus actually rise from the dead?

In the 1930's, a man trained in law—Frank Morison
—decided that he would try to solve the question of the
resurrection once and for all. He chose to study the last
seven days of Jesus' life to get at just why Jesus had to
die a cruel death at the hands of the Romans, what
Jesus Himself thought of the entire situation and how
He behaved during the trial and execution.

In the beginning, Morison set out to "disprove" the
resurrection but he kept running into questions he
could not answer unless he would accept the fact of the
resurrection. Morison finished writing his book fully
convinced that Jesus of Nazareth had died on the cross
and three days later He did rise from the dead.

The title of Morison's book asks a key question that
no one has answered satisfactorily yet: *Who Moved the
Stone?** Who did move the gigantic stone placed in
front of the tomb of Jesus, which was guarded by a
group of crack Roman soldiers? Why didn't the Jewish
authorities simply produce Jesus' body in order to quiet
all of the "silly talk about His rising from the dead"?

*Who Moved the Stone? Frank Morison. Copyright 1930, Faber and
Faber Limited, published in paperback edition in the U.S. in 1962
by Barnes and Noble, Inc.

Another question that is hard to answer is: How did Christianity become the vital faith of so many people in such a short time if it was based on a colossal lie? Perhaps some of the disciples would have been willing to die for a lie, but it is hard to believe that *all* of them would have died (many of them by violent deaths, according to tradition) for Christianity if it were nothing but a hoax.

There is also this question: What hope would the disciples have had—what purpose would they have had —in proclaiming such powerful messages about the resurrection if there had been no resurrection? What would be their purpose in preaching a lie or in preaching about something of which they were not even sure?

Is Jesus Christ mentioned in any historical writings besides the Bible?

Josephus Flavius, famed Jewish historian and contemporary of Jesus, wrote in Chapter 18 of his *Antiquities* about a man named Jesus, ". . . a wise man . . . a doer of marvelous deeds . . . (who) led away many Jews and also many Greeks. This man was the Christ. And when Pilate had condemned him to the cross . . . those who had loved him at first did not cease; for he appeared to them on the third day alive again . . . and even now the tribe of Christians, so named after him, has not yet died out."

In the British Museum is a letter written in the first century by a Syrian, Mara Bar-Serapion, who says, "What advantage did the Jews gain from executing their wise king (Jesus)?" Cornelius Tacitus, major Roman historian of the first century, records the burning of Rome in A.D. 64 and how Nero made scapegoats of ". . . a class of men, loathed for their vices . . . Christians. Christus, from whom they got their name, had

**THE BRIDGES ARE THERE . . .
HOW MANY HAVE YOU CROSSED?**

been executed by sentence of the procurator Pontius
Pilate . . ."*

What difference does it make if you want to believe Jesus was "only a man" and not God?

If Christ was only a man, the incarnation (God
becoming man) never really happened, and God never
did climax His acts of revelation in Jesus Christ. A
human Jesus leaves you with nothing more than a
system of ethics, but no real hope for your sins and no
final assurance that you can know God personally. In
essence, you are left with the Scriptures, but they are
Scriptures that teach the terrible standards of the law to
which no man can attain. As Paul has pointed out, the
law (the Ten Commandments) is our "schoolmaster,"
but its purpose is to bring us to Jesus Christ. (See Gal.
3:24.)

The law shows us how imperfect we are and how
much we are in need of a Saviour. The New Testament
makes it clear that Christ and God are the same. We

*For detailed information on mention of Christ in early Jewish writ-
ings and Gentile histories, see The New Testament Documents: Are
They Reliable?, F. F. Bruce, W. B. Eerdmans, 1943, pp. 100-120.

know that only God can forgive sins. Yet, we find Christ forgiving sins (see, for example, Mark 2:5,10; Luke 7:47-49). Only God can give eternal life, yet Christ promises eternal life (John 10:28). Jesus even goes on to say that He is life itself (John 14:6).

If Jesus is not truly God, Christianity is built on a gigantic lie. A mere man cannot forgive sins and impart eternal life.

God has bridged the gap between Himself and man in at least three ways. He reveals Himself in nature. He reveals Himself in His written Word. Most important, however, God reveals Himself completely in Jesus Christ, the living Word. Nature, the Bible and Christ are all bridges between man and God, bridges that span the gap caused by man's sin and love of darkness, rather than light (John 3:19). The bridges are there, *but it still takes personal faith to cross them.*

Have you crossed any of these bridges? Keep in mind that nature and the Bible take you only part of the way. The final—most important—span is Jesus Christ Himself.

For further reading

Paperbacks

Your God Is Too Small, J. B. Phillips, The Macmillan Company, 1961. See especially Part 2, pp. 63-120.

Who Moved the Stone? Frank Morison, Barnes and Noble, Inc., 1962. Contains 192 pages that record how a man set out to disprove the resurrection and ended writing his book as a believer in Jesus Christ.

Hardbacks

The Lord from Heaven, Leon Morris, Wm. B. Eerdmans Publishing Co., 1958. Contains 112 pages that probe the meaning of the Person of Christ and the two great truths—that Jesus was God and that He was man.

The Gospel of John, Vol. 1, from the Daily Study Bible Series, edited by William Barclay, Westminster Press, 1955. See pages 1-49.

CHAPTER 3

What's so special about the Bible?

The Bible is the most widely read book of all time. It has been translated into every major (and almost every minor) language. The Bible has an equally strong appeal to nuclear physicists and Auca Indians. Yet, in spite of its immense popularity, the Bible is also the most widely attacked book ever written.

In the 20th century, criticism of the Bible has not only grown from outside of Christianity, but also from within it! Today there are many liberal thinkers being paid to be ministers and seminary teachers who spend much of their time writing and publishing articles to discredit the Bible. Many of these men say that the Bible is merely a collection of stories and superstitions which "contain" the teaching of God. These men claim to be able to sort out truth from what they call fiction in the Bible, but few of them ever seem to agree with one another.

Faced with all of this high-sounding criticism of the Bible, the Christian today asks:

How do I know that the Bible is not just another man-made book?

The Bible itself claims to be the Word of God. Within its pages are many claims to this effect. Paul wrote to Timothy that "All scripture is given by inspiration of God, and is profitable for doctrine, for reproof, for correction, for instruction in righteousness" (II Tim. 3:16). Peter also wrote that ". . . prophecy came not in old time by the will of man; but holy men of God spake as they were moved by the Holy Ghost" (II Peter 1:21).

One of the major doctrines of the Bible is that the Bible itself is, in its entirety, the Word of God. Statements, such as "God said," and "the word of the Lord," occur hundreds and even thousands of times in the Bible. There are 2700 such statements in the Old Testament alone, all of which make direct claim that the Bible is the Word of God.

The Bible is either what these writers claim it is—God's Word to man—or these writers were one of two things: deluded or deceitful. Just as there is no middle ground concerning Christ's deity, there is no middle ground on the inspiration of Scripture. Either it is God's Word or it is only man's word. Some people do not believe that the Bible is inspired, but they think it is "great literature" or that it contains great moral truth. It is hard to see, however, how great literature or moral truth could contain deliberate lies or stupid mistakes.

What does "inspiration of the Bible" really mean?

In II Tim. 3:16, the Greek word used for "inspiration" literally means "God-breathed." Conservative, orthodox Christians believe in the "verbal plenary inspiration" of Scripture, that is, the full and complete inspiration of all the Bible. This means that God so moved upon the minds and abilities of the writers that

INSPIRATION DOESN'T MEAN THE WRITERS OF SCRIPTURE WERE WIRED FOR MECHANICAL DICTATION

the words they used expressed the thoughts and the will of God. In other words, the superintendency of the Holy Spirit rendered the writers of Scripture infallible in their communication of truth and inerrant in their literary productions. That's what Scripture means when it says, "holy men of God ... were moved by the Holy Ghost" (II Peter 1:21).

Some critics of the Bible claim that to hold to verbal plenary inspiration of Scripture means you are saying that God dictated every word and every punctuation mark to men who were mere "mechanical stenographers" who dutifully took it all down.

A simple reading of Scripture proves that "the mechanical dictation" viewpoint is without basis. The personality and style of each writer are most evident. While it is true that parts of the Bible were "dictated" (the Ten Commandments, for example), for the most part "holy men of God ... were moved by the Holy Ghost" to write holy Scripture (II Peter 1:21). The writers of Scripture were more than "stenographers." God allowed them their individuality and creativity, but the point is that He worked *through them* to bring His revelation to man—the Bible—into being.

What other evidence can we find in the Bible to "prove" it is God's inspired Word?

Despite dozens of authors and centuries in its writing, the Bible's unity of theme and purpose points to a supernatural guiding power. Think about it for yourself.

The entire Bible represents the inspired efforts of at least 40 men who wrote over a period of 1500 years. Yet, there is unity of theme, consistency of concepts, logical development, and agreement in doctrine. True, critics have pointed out what they believe to be errors,* but so far no critic has found any major damaging inconsistency in the Bible.

Other evidence for the inspiration of the Bible includes hundreds of prophecies that have been fulfilled to the letter (see Chapter 5) and a growing number of archaeological discoveries that prove the Bible's historical accuracy (see Chapter 6).

Men have used the Bible's teachings on mercy, justice and ethics to guide their social development. It is certainly accurate to say that Western civilization is a product of the Bible and Christianity. England and the United States are both great nations today, because they are founded on principles contained in Scripture.

The fact that men have used the Bible as a basis for social laws and political organization does not in itself prove that the Scriptures are the inspired Word of God. But to refer to a point made earlier, the Bible itself

*When Christians say they believe the Bible is inerrant, they do not mean the authorized King James version or any other translation of Scripture is inerrant. While these translations are good, there are errors in them. As J. Gresham Machen has pointed out, believers in the inspiration of the Bible do not believe that the scribes who made copies of the manuscripts were inspired. The writers of Biblical books were inspired and only the original autographs, that is, the books as they came from the pens of the inspired writers, were produced with the supernatural influence and guidance of the Holy Spirit.

NO TRANSLATION OR VERSION
OF THE BIBLE IS INERRANT . . .
BUT THE ORIGINAL MANUSCRIPTS WERE.

41

claims to be the inspired Word of God—some 2700 times in the Old Testament alone. The skeptic is left with the question: How could a book influence men for so much good and be a colossal lie in regard to its divine authorship?

Despite the evidence for the inspiration of Scripture, certain critics are unconvinced. They still ask:

On whose authority can you accept the Bible as the inspired Word of God?

Behind this question lies the attitude of our day. This attitude questions all absolutes and maintains that all truth is relative because nothing can be known for sure. When dealing with this kind of rationalistic thinking,* it does little good to quote church authorities or even the great theologians of the past.

Fortunately, the Christian is not left with the option of quoting only human authority concerning inspiration of the Bible. He can quote God Himself—Jesus Christ.

The New Testament makes it clear that Christ believed that the Scriptures are the Word of God. For example, Christ believed in the permanence of the Scriptures, for He said, with all earnestness, "... Every law in the Book will continue until its purpose is achieved" (Matt. 5:18, *Living Gospels*). Jesus also believed that all of Scripture is sacred. That is what He meant when He said "... the scripture cannot be broken" (John 10:35).

Jesus also believed that the Scriptures were the final authority for His earthly life and for lives of all men.

---

*Rationalism was the philosophy that arose during the seventeenth and eighteenth centuries with the rise of natural science and an increasing skepticism about the supernatural. If a non-Christian is a "rationalist," it does not follow that all Christians are irrational. A Christian can be just as rational as anyone else in the sense that he thinks clearly with the evidence at hand. But a rationalist, in a philosophical sense, is one who comes to the evidence with the presupposed bias that the supernatural is impossible and that everything can be explained in natural terms.

For example, He corrected the Pharisees, who had substituted their man-made rules and traditions for genuine worhsip of God when He told them that Isaiah the prophet had described them very well by writing, "... 'these people speak very prettily about the Lord, but they have no love for him at all. Their worship is a farce ...'" (Mark 7:7, *Living Gospels*).

Jesus used Scripture authoritatively on many other occasions: when tempted by Satan (Matt. 4:1-10); when teaching about His Messiahship (Luke 4:16-21); and especially during the final weeks and days before the cross, when He knew what He must do in order that "... the scriptures be fulfilled ..." (see Luke 18:31; Matt. 26:54).

Even a casual reading of the Gospels proves without a doubt that Jesus believed that the Scriptures were infallible. Read the passages listed above and see for yourself. For additional references, see John 5:29-47; Matt. 12:40; Luke 24:44.

Can you "believe in Christ" but not in the inspiration of the Bible?

There are people today who say that they believe in Jesus Christ, but they don't believe that the Scriptures are the inspired Word of God. To hold this point of view puts you in an inconsistent position. It is difficult to see how a person can believe in Christ without believing in the Scriptures, because the Scriptures are the one source of specific and detailed information about Him.

As Dr. Kenneth Kantzer, Dean of Trinity Seminary, has pointed out, "The basic question about the inspiration and authority of Scripture is 'what do you think of Christ?' If we accept Him as Lord, it's consistent to submit to His teaching on the complete authority of Scripture. To accept Christ's Lordship and at the same

I believe in Christ, but I can't buy the idea of an inspired Bible.

IS THIS A CONSISTENT VIEWPOINT? WHY?

time to reject the inspiration and authority of the Bible is inconsistent."[*]

What about the idea that the Bible is "inspiring, but not inspired"?

Modern theologians (liberals and those of the neo-orthodox school) do not hold the verbal plenary view of inspiration. Although fading in influence, liberals have typically said that the Bible is inspired at a human level, but not a divine one. They say the Bible is inspiring because it makes an impression upon the minds of men as other great works of human literature have done. But, their distrust of the Bible's accuracy causes them to deny that Scripture is actually the inspired Word of God.

Neo-orthodox theologians hold a somewhat different position and are known for saying that the Bible "contains the Word of God." The neo-orthodox thinker attempts to separate God's "real message" from the "mistakes and superstitions" which were added to it by its writers. They say if one can accomplish this feat, he can find out what God is really saying. In addition, the neo-orthodox thinker claims that the Bible is inspired when and how it speaks to the individual. This puts the entire matter on a subjective basis and leaves Scripture without any real authority or power.

[*]From "Christ and Scripture," Dr. Kenneth S. Kantzer, His, Copyright Inter-Varsity Christian Fellowship, 1965.

The Bible contains the Word of God . . . that is, when it speaks to me.

NEO ORTHODOXY HOLDS THIS VIEW OF SCRIPTURE

Are there myths in the Bible?

Critics of the Bible, both past and present, believe that Scripture is made up of many myths. They define "myth" as "a story which many people have come to believe is true, but which is not based on actual fact."

Modern criticism of the Bible came into its own in the eighteenth century with the dawn of the "age of reason." "Higher criticism" of the Bible became the order of the day as outstanding intellectuals attacked the inspiration of Scripture and denied its supernatural and miraculous elements.*

Higher criticism led to many fanciful theories about Scripture. For example, the "documentary hypothesis" claimed that Moses did not write the Pentateuch (first five books of the Bible). Various unknown writers, living after Moses, were supposed to have written these books. These anonymous authors were identified by certain characteristics in the documents, especially the name they used for God.

One of the best known systems of this kind was J-E-D-P, which was popularized by such scholars as H. K. Graf (1866). According to Graf, 'J' documents, using the name Jehovah for God, were the earliest ones

*Higher criticism actually means a study of the date, authorship, place and circumstances of composition, as well as purpose and nature of individual Biblical books. Higher criticism can be used by the conservative orthodox scholar to deepen his understanding of inspired Scripture, but in popular parlance, the term "higher criticism" is usually used to describe the critic who denies the inspiration of Scripture.

in the Pentateuch. They were followed by the 'E' documents, which used the name Elohim. 'D' documents were next and were associated with the book of Deuteronomy. 'P' documents were of the latest origin and were supposedly penned by certain Israelite priests.

In the 1870's, Julius Wellhausen built on the documentary approach that had been developed by Graf and other scholars before him. Wellhausen called his particular view the "developmental hypothesis."

According to Wellhausen, Moses knew nothing of one God because he lived too early for such a lofty concept. Moses was supposed to have persuaded Israel to choose one of their idols and cleave to it. In this way, "Jehovah" became a tribal god, which the Jews later claimed was greater than the gods of other nations. Still later, during the times of Amos and Hosea, Jehovah became the "only God" and monotheism fully evolved.

The developmental hypothesis reigned supreme until the 1920's, but today it is disregarded by most scholars. Advanced Biblical scholarship coupled with numerous archaeological discoveries has shown that the higher criticism of Scripture was based on limited information and biased presupposition. In addition, two World Wars have done much to dampen the evolutionary conception of man (the idea that man is getting better and better), which is the foundation of much higher critical thinking.

Although the developmental hypothesis of Wellhausen is discredited, the documentary theories concerning the Old Testament are still held today by scholars who refuse to accept the trustworthiness and inspiration of Scripture. In addition, they apply similar methods of higher criticism to the New Testament. In fact, modern critics have centered a great deal of attention on the New Testament in recent years.

Liberalism has been replaced today in some circles by neo-orthodoxy and existentialism, viewpoints that recognize man's sin but that still deny the historical accuracy and inspiration of Scripture. Karl Barth (founder of neo-orthodoxy in 1919), Emil Brunner and Rudolph Bultmann (existential demythologizer of Scripture) are prime examples of influential 20th century theologians.

These modern theologians believe that the New Testament is a product of myths and legends that grew up in the early church after Jesus' crucifixion. They believe that the "Jesus of history" was a simple itinerant preacher who had popular appeal to the masses but who ran afoul of the Roman authorities and was tragically martyred for his revolutionary views. The Neo-orthodox thinkers believe that such ideas as the deity of Christ and His resurrection from the dead are "theological trimmings" that were added by writers of the New Testament in a burst of mystical religious fervor.

The conservative Bible scholar answers this charge by asking: just how long does it take for myths to become believed by a large number of people? Clark Pinnock points out that myths take centuries to develop. German folklore, for example, required hundreds of years. The Gospel, however, exploded into life suddenly and completely as people who had known Jesus reported what they had seen and heard.*

While there is little question that higher critics are learned men, there is also little question that they base their arguments on the same presupposition of the 19th century critics: disbelief in the supernatural. As C. S. Lewis observes, however, this skepticism about the supernatural is a concept that such critics bring to their study of the Bible, not one they have learned from it.

*"The Case Against Form Criticism," Clark Pinnock, **Christianity Today**, July 16, 1965, p. 13.

HIGHER CRITICS APPROACH THE BIBLE
WITH THE PRESUPPOSITION
THAT THE SUPERNATURAL IS IMPOSSIBLE

They speak as men obviously influenced by the spirit of
their times, an age of skepticism and rationalistic cock-
sureness that modern science can find all the answers.*

While the claims and credentials of higher critics are
impressive, the Christian remains unconvinced about
their infallibility. Higher critics were proven wrong in
the late 19th and early 20th centuries. They are still
being challenged today on objective grounds by conservative scholars.

The Christian need make no apology for believing
the Bible is the inspired Word of God, (not myth) and
reliable history (not legends).

Why is the Bible attacked so viciously by certain critics?

Although many of these critics would deny it, the
answer is essentially a moral issue. The Bible tells the
age-old truth about man—that he is a sinner in need of
a Saviour. The Bible claims (and history has borne it
out precisely) that man is incapable of consistently
doing anything that is morally and spiritually right.
Man may "do all right for awhile." He may build a
civilization and make great progress in certain areas,

*See **Christian Reflections**, C. S. Lewis, edited by Walter Hooper,
Eerdman's, 1967, pp. 152-166.

but ultimately man's moral and spiritual weaknesses come to the surface, often in the form of war, killing, cruelty, prejudice, ignorance, disease and death.

Sinful men, especially those inclined to embrace the humanistic idea that man is evolving toward perfection, do not want to hear the truth that is in the Bible. They put forth an enormous effort to discredit the Scriptures and label them untrustworthy. These attacks on the Bible are often done in a most sophisticated and intellectual way, which can sound quite convincing in print or in the academic classroom. But behind the impressive intellectual front is a basic attitude of rebellion toward God and basic pride in man and what man has accomplished.*

No other book, even writings of other religions, has been attacked so vigorously for so long a period of time. These attacks in themselves are evidence of the inspiration of Scripture. Why attack something so vociferously unless you really fear that it contains the truth?

How can a Christian answer Bible critics?

First, realize that few people really know what the Bible actually says. Most men who criticize the Bible, except for a few scholars, are rather ignorant of the Scriptures. When asked to produce a real "inconsistency" they are unable to do so. Therefore, in the words of the athletic world, the best defense is good offense. The Christian should know his Bible inside and out. There is no more powerful answer for critics than to be

*There is no intention here to stereotype all neo-orthodox and existentialist scholars as "immoral" or "humanistic." Many of today's higher critics of Scripture admit that man is a sinner, but their basic distrust of the Bible as reliable history (a hangover from liberalism) causes them to treat Scripture as a human document. These critics claim that the Bible is subject to error and in need of "interpretation" or "demythologizing" in order to find the real "theological truth." This approach to the Bible plays into the hands of the rationalists and humanists who refuse to accept the Bible's judgment on man as a sinner in need of a Saviour.

able to "cite chapter and verse" from the very book that they are criticizing.

The Bible has the power to win men and women to Jesus Christ, far more power than any brilliant film, profound book or clever argument. (See Heb. 4:12; Rom. 1:16.)

Secondly, realize that criticisms are based on a basic presupposition. The battle-cry of the rationalist is, "Miracles do not happen." The Christian's answer is that miracles do happen because the Bible plainly records these supernatural events. Also, where is the critic of Scripture who has ever proved to be so infallible that he can explain everything that happens in this world by a purely rational and naturalistic means?

Isn't the Bible a difficult book? How can I read it and understand it?

Much of the difficulty in Bible reading disappears when you use a modern up-to-date translation or paraphrase. Any number of these are on the market and can revolutionize your understanding of Scripture.

In addition, here are some other practical ways to get more out of your Bible reading:*

1. Read expectantly and thoughtfully, asking, "what is God's message to me today? What does this passage teach me to believe? To become?"

2. Read with imagination, unhurriedly, picturing the scene and seeing the characters as living people.

3. Use standard helps such as commentaries, Bible dictionaries and concordance (as well as a good modern translation of the Scripture).

4. Do not be disturbed if there are some passages you do not understand. As someone has said, "It's not the

*Adapted from "How to Read the Bible," Dr. Francis C. Stifler, American Bible Society.

parts of the Bible I can't understand that bother me, it's the parts that I *do* understand."

5. Keep a record of what you read and the impressions you receive. Also memorize helpful passages— that's right *memorize them*. Emphasis on Bible memorization seems to have declined in recent years. The common concept is that memorizing Scripture is "Mickey Mouse" and something little kids do to earn colored stickers. In addition there's the charge that "rote memorizing isn't really learning."

Most of these complaints are hangovers from childhood, when individuals were forced (or bribed) into rattling off a string of Bible verses they didn't really understand. But these excuses just don't hold water. The whole purpose of Bible memorizing is to commit to memory the verses that do have meaning. In other words the person who can think for himself memorizes verses because he *wants* to—because they have *particular value* to him.

Most important of all for gaining a good understanding of the Bible is to know the Author, that is, the One who inspired it. In other words, believe on Jesus Christ as Saviour and Lord of your life. When Christ is in your life you have the guidance of the Holy Spirit. Paul writes in I Corinthians that it is necessary to have the Holy Spirit in order to know the wisdom of God and understand His Word.

"... the unspiritual man (the person who does not know Christ as Saviour) simply can't accept the matters which the Spirit deals with—they just don't make sense, for, after all you must be spiritual to see spiritual things. The spiritual man, on the other hand, has an insight into the meaning of everything, though his insight may baffle the man of the world" (I Cor. 2:14,15, *Phillips Translation*).

Why all the fuss about reading the Bible? Isn't living the Christian life what really counts?

Living the Christian life is definitely what counts, but the question is, how do you learn to do this except by looking into the source of information on what the Christian life is all about?

One way of looking at the Bible is to see it as the rudder for your life. During World War II the Nazis had a battleship—the Bismarck—considered to be the most powerful fighting ship ever built by man. In addition, she was considered unsinkable because of a honeycomb of watertight compartments below her decks.

On the afternoon of May 21, 1941, the Bismarck was sighted by a British reconnaissance plane in the North Atlantic. Immediately, ships from the Royal British Navy sped to the scene. The Bismarck was attacked first by the H.M.S. Hood, Britain's largest warship. In ten minutes the Hood was headed for the bottom of the sea, victim of the Bismarck's awesome fire power.

As the Bismarck headed south past the British Isles, she was attacked by British torpedo bombers, but apparently the torpedoes had little effect. More British ships were closing in. It was obvious the Bismarck was trying to make a port on the French coast that was controlled by the German army. Then, to the astonishment of everyone, the Bismarck suddenly swung around and reentered the area where the British ships were massed in greatest strength. At the same time she began to steer an erratic zigzag course.

British naval officers could think of only one explanation. A torpedo had damaged her rudder after all. The British Navy closed in with everything it had, and because she lacked a rudder, the "unsinkable" Bismarck was sunk.*

The application is obvious. Many Christians appar-

*Adapted from "Sunk," His magazine, November, 1960, p. 31.

ently seem to have "superior spiritual fire power" and great ability that could be used for Christ. Yet these very people often wind up "sunk," or they run aground on the rocks of apathy, doubt and lukewarm indifference to the Lord. Why? Their "rudders" are out of commission.

The Christian's rudder is his regular communion with God which he has through reading the Bible and talking with his Lord. *There is absolutely no substitute for this.* Most Christians will piously agree that "they should read the Bible and pray" but all too many of them never follow through and actually do it. Is it any wonder then that books have to be written to help Christians know why the Bible is inspired? The evidence for the inspiration of Scripture is there. But evidence is useless unless it is examined and tested and experienced.

Too many Christians are "cutting corners" on Bible study (and more important, in spending time with Christ) because they think that somehow their pastor or Bible teacher can "make up the difference" by spoon feeding them once a week. They try to "live the Christian life" but they are getting their fuel second hand and their rudders are rusty and practically useless.

How is *your* rudder? Only you can answer that question, and in the answer to that question lies the

TOO MANY CHRISTIANS
DEPEND ON WEEKLY SPOON
FEEDING FOR THEIR SPIRITUAL NOURISHMENT

answer to the question that opened this chapter: "What's so special about the Bible?"

For further reading

Paperbacks

Christianity and Liberalism, J. Gresham Machen, Wm. B. Eerdmans Publishing Co., 1923. See Chapter 4 "The Bible."

The New Testament Documents, Are They Reliable?, F. F. Bruce, W. B. Eerdmans Publishing Co., 1943. Contains 113 pages of scholarly but very readable information substantiating the trustworthiness of the New Testament.

The Wonder of the Word, Gwynn McLendon Day, Moody Press, 1957, original copyright by Fleming H. Revell Co. Contains 255 pages packed with information, evidence and testimonies concerning the inspiration of Scripture.

Is the Higher Criticism Scholarly? Robert Dick Wilson, The Sunday School Times, 1922. A brief booklet of 62 pages by one of the leading Old Testament scholars of the early 20th century who mastered some 26 languages while making a life-long study of Scripture that was devoted in great part to refuting the claims of liberal higher criticism of the Bible.

Hardbacks

The Books and the Parchments, F. F. Bruce, Fleming H. Revell Co., 1950. Contains 287 pages designed to help the layman study how the Bible has come down to present day believers from the original manuscripts.

Can I Trust My Bible?, Moody Press, 1963. A 190-page compilation of writings by eight scholars on inspiration of Scripture, the canon, the reliability and historical accuracy of the Old and New Testaments.

General Biblical Introduction, H. S. Miller, Word-Bearer Press, 1940. Contains 422 pages done in standard textbook outline style but loaded with valuable information and condensed into readable and easily digested sections.

A Scientific Investigation of the Old Testament, Robert Dick Wilson, the Sunday School Times Co., 1926. Contains 225 pages examining the evidence related to the text, grammar, vocabulary, history, and religion of the Old Testament.

The Bible, Science and Creation, S. Maxwell Coder and George F. Howe, Moody Press, 1965. See chapters 1 and 2 on "The Inspiration of the Bible," also chapter 3, "Difficulties in the Bible."

CHAPTER 4

Are the right books in the Bible?

As Chapter 3 pointed out, the Bible was written by men who were moved by the Holy Ghost to write what God intended to be written. But the question then comes up: "How were the books of the Bible *chosen*? Just who decided on what was inspired and what was not?"

The collection of Biblical books in the Old and New Testaments is called the "canon." The word, canon, means a "standard or measuring rod." Christians consider the "canon of Scripture" their final authority for faith and practice.

The question might be asked, "Why worry about the canon or how it was formed? It was done a long time ago and what difference does it make anyway?" Many people have a vague notion that the Bible is the product of ignorance and superstition. The Christian may sometimes have an opportunity to say something to a doubter concerning these points, but he will only have something to say if he actually knows something about the canon and how it was formed.

Who compiled the Old and New Testaments and how did they go about it?

The canon of the Old Testament was collected by the Jews, and the New Testament canon was collected by Christians in the early church during the first through third centuries. As for how these compilers of Scripture were guided, the Christian holds that they were directed in exactly the same way as were writers of holy Scripture—by the Holy Spirit.

An absolutely essential point is that the canon was chosen by men of faith, but their minds were illuminated by the Holy Spirit to help them discern truth from error. Did they choose the books of the Bible by playing "blind man's buff" with a stack of scrolls? The record shows that they used their reason, their intelligence and many stringent tests to decide if a book really belonged in holy Scripture.

What tests were used to decide the inspiration of Old Testament books?

The Old Testament canon includes the 39 books found in today's Protestant Bibles. These 39 books divide into four major sections: Law, History, Poetry, and Prophets. In Biblical times, including the days of Christ's earthly ministry, the Hebrew Old Testament contained precisely these same 39 books, but they were arranged in a different number—24—and also in a different order with three main sections: the Law, the Prophets and the Writings. The Hebrew Old Testament totaled out at 24 (in some cases 22) books, because certain books were grouped together as one book. (See chart, p. 57, comparing today's Protestant Old Testament with the Hebrew Old Testament used during the time of Christ and long before.)

During the time when Old Testament Scripture was

COMPARISON OF HEBREW OLD TESTAMENT AND PROTESTANT OLD TESTAMENT

THE HEBREW OLD TESTAMENT	THE PROTESTANT OLD TESTAMENT
THE LAW:	Genesis
Genesis	Exodus
Exodus	Leviticus
Leviticus	Numbers
Numbers	Deuteronomy
Deuteronomy	Joshua
	Judges
THE PROPHETS:	Ruth
Joshua	I Samuel
Judges	II Samuel
Samuel	I Kings
Kings	II Kings
Isaiah	I Chronicles
Jeremiah	II Chronicles
Ezekiel	Ezra
The Book of the Twelve	Nehemiah
(Hosea to Malachi)	Esther
	Job
THE WRITINGS:	Psalms
Psalms	Proverbs
Proverbs	Ecclesiastes
Job	Song of Solomon
Song of Songs	Isaiah
Ruth	Jeremiah
Lamentations	Lamentations
Ecclesiastes	Ezekiel
Esther	Daniel
Daniel	Hosea
Ezra–Nehemiah	Joel
Chronicles	Amos
	Obadiah
	Jonah
	Micah
	Nahum
	Habakkuk
	Zephaniah
	Haggai
	Zechariah
	Malachi

The Hebrew Old Testament condenses the arrangements of books to 24, as shown above. In some cases, the Jews limited the list to 22 by combining Ruth with Judges and Lamentations with Jeremiah. See quote by Josephus on p. 58.

being written (from the days of Moses on), the Jews used two major tests to decide if a book was genuine holy writ. First, was it written by a prophet or someone with the gift of prophecy? Moses was considered by the Jews to be a prophet, as were such men as Isaiah and Ezekiel. Other Jewish leaders, while not holding the official rank of prophet, were still recognized as possessors of prophetic powers. Such men included Daniel, a government official in Babylon; Solomon and David, kings of Israel; Ezra, a scribe; Nehemiah, a civil governor.*

Another key test was the acceptance and use of Old Testament books by the Hebrew people. The Jews looked on the Old Testament books as sacred Scripture from the very time they were written.

Just when all the books of the Old Testament were written is uncertain, but conservative scholars believe that all of Old Testament Scripture was completed by no later than 425 B.C. with the book of Malachi, the last of the Old Testament prophets.**

The liberal higher critic sees no divine inspiration in the Old Testament. He claims the Old Testament is a compilation of writings done at three different times following the exile of the Hebrew nation in Babylon and finally finished about 100 to 200 A.D. (Review other information on higher criticism in Chapter 3.)

Conservative Bible scholars feel there is ample evidence to counter the liberal higher critical view. For example, there is the writing of Josephus, the famed Jewish historian. In a paper written around 100 A.D., Josephus plainly states that all the sacred books of the Jews (the Old Testament) were written between the time of Moses and the days of Artaxerxes I (a king of Persia who reigned from 465 to 424 B.C.). Part of Josephus' statement reads as follows:

"For we have not an innumerable multitude of books among us, disagreeing from and contradicting one another (as the Greeks have), but only 22 books, which contain the record of all time; which are justly believed to be divine. And of these, five are the books of Moses, which contain the laws and the traditions from the origin of mankind till his (Moses') death. This interval of time is a little short of 3000 years. But as to the time from the death of Moses till

*Unger's Bible Dictionary, Merrill F. Unger. Copyright 1957, Moody Bible Institute, p. 177.
**General Biblical Introduction, H. S. Miller, The Word-Bearer Press. Copyright 1940, p. 103.

the reign of Artaxerxes, king of Persia, who reigned after Xerxes, the prophets who were after Moses wrote down what was done in their time in 13 books. The remaining four books contain hymns to God and precepts for the conduct of human life . . . no one has been so bold as either to add anything to them, to take anything from them, or to make any change in them . . . (Josephus, *Against Apion,* I, 8).*

Actually, the most authoritative evidence that the Christian has for the inspiration of the Old Testament canon are the words of Christ Himself. Christ recognized the Scriptures as the inspired Word of God. See, for example, John 10:34; Matt. 5:18; John 5:39. Also review Christ's view of the Scripture in Chapter 3.

In Luke 24:44, Christ makes a direct reference to the three sections of the Hebrew Old Testament canon, the Law, the Prophets and the Psalms. On this occasion, He appeared to His disciples following the resurrection to tell them how everything written about Him in the Law of Moses and the Prophets and the Psalms must be fulfilled. Christ was obviously referring to the Old Testament Scriptures that were in existence at that time and this reference is authoritative evidence that Christ Himself knew, respected and used the Old Testament.

What tests were used to decide the inspiration of New Testament books?

As Christianity spread throughout the Roman Empire in the first century, it became apparent that a written gospel record was necessary for the sake of clear and accurate communication. The four Gospels, plus the rest of the New Testament books, were all written between 50 and 100 A.D., all by apostles (men from among Christ's original disciples, plus Paul) or by writers closely associated with apostles. Mark, for exam-

*General Biblical Introduction, H. S. Miller. The Word-Bearer Press. Copyright 1940, p. 104.

CHIEF TESTS FOR INSPIRATION

ple, used Peter as his chief source for his Gospel. Luke, who wrote the book of Acts as well as the Gospel bearing his name, was a close companion of Paul.

The rise of heresy in the early church also had much to do with the formulation of the New Testament canon. The Gnostics (see Chapter 2), who taught a strange mixture of Christian doctrine and pagan philosophy, began developing their own "sacred writings" by compiling certain apostolic books and then editing them to suit their own ideas.

Tests to determine genuine New Testament Scripture included the following:

Apostolic authorship and authority was the chief test of all. The men who had lived with Christ and who had seen Him and had talked with Him following His resurrection had unique authority and power. In order for a New Testament book to be considered thoroughly genuine, it had to be recognized by members of the early church as truly apostolic. To be apostolic, the book had to be directly written by an apostle or written by someone (such as Mark or Luke) who had associated closely with the apostles.

Use of the books in Christian churches and by church

60

leaders was a chief method of determining a book's apostolic genuineness. Church fathers such as Polycarp, Justin Martyr, Tertullian, Origen, Eusebius, Athanasius, Jerome and Augustine all used the inspired apostolic writings. They led in the slow and gradual collection of the New Testament canon over the first four centuries A.D.

Keep in mind, however, that the church leaders did not pick out books they thought were genuine and force them on passive Christian church members. The books were tested through a steady usage and the canon gradually emerged through the combined conviction of the church leaders and church members who worked in harmony.

The New Testament canon was not officially decreed by any church council, although several church councils met to recognize the views of the people and the existence of the collected New Testament canon. The complete New Testament canon of 27 books was closed by the end of the fourth century.

Other tests to find inspired New Testament books included agreement with correct Christian doctrine and power to build up believers in the Christian faith. Some New Testament apocryphal books were read in the churches, but were later discarded because they taught doctrines differing from the essential Christian rule of faith based on the death and resurrection of Christ or because they were discovered to not be of apostolic origin. (For more on the apocrypha, see pp. 62-64.)

While all these tests were important, one other test was still far more vital: the guiding power of the Holy Spirit. The Christian has no "absolute proof" that all the books in the canon are the ones that belong there. The Christian looks at the evidence, which is substantial and convincing, but in the final analysis, the Christian must trust in Christ's promise to His apostles in John 16:13:

". . . the Spirit of truth will guide you into all truth . . . and he will show you things to come."

When Christ promised the apostles that they would be guided by His Holy Spirit into all truth, He indirectly put His stamp of approval on the New Testament writings that the apostles would go on to produce. John 16 paves the way for the words and writings of the apostles, who were commissioned by Christ and then moved by the Holy Spirit to declare the gospel throughout the world.

What are the apocryphal books and why aren't they included in the canon of Scripture?

The word "apocrypha" means "hidden or concealed." Apocryphal books are secret documents, written for a certain "in group" (sometimes a heretical sect of some kind). From this concept of something secretive or undercover came a second meaning that was applied to certain books which, according to some people, belonged in the canons of the Old and New Testaments.

There were 14 Old Testament apocryphal books: 1 Esdras; 2 Esdras; Tobit; Judith; The Rest of Esther; The Wisdom of Solomon; Ecclesiasticus; Baruch, with the Epistle of Jeremiah; The Song of the Three Holy Children; The History of Susanna; Bell and the Dragon; The Prayer of Manasses; 1 Maccabees; 2 Maccabees.

Although the Old Testament apocryphal books contain some useful historical material and a wide range of ethical instructions they were not allowed in the Old Testament canon for many reasons.

For example, apocryphal books were written long after the Old Testament canon was closed (that is, after the last of the prophetic utterances were made by Malachi in 425 B.C.). Because of when they were written, apocryphal books lacked the prophetic quality that was a crucial test of inspired Scripture as far as the Old Testament was concerned.

The apocryphal books are never quoted in the New Testament, by Jesus Christ or by any New Testament writer. Josephus also excluded them when he limited the number of divinely inspired books to 22 (see p. 58).

Divine inspiration is not claimed by any of the apocryphal writers, and in fact, some of the writers disclaim inspiration.

Although some of the apocryphal books have value, a great deal of apocryphal writing contains errors of fact and teach doctrines and ethics that are contrary to inspired Scripture. For example, lying is acceptable when the end justifies the means. Suicide and assassination are justified and prayers for the dead are also taught. Much apocryphal literature contains absurdities and so-called miracles that border on the grotesque and silly. No apocryphal book ever found its way into the Jewish canon.

Certain apochryphal books were also associated with the New Testament, some 15 in fact: The Teaching of the Twelve Apostles Didache; The Epistle of Barnabas; The First Epistle of Clement; The Second Epistle of Clement; The Shepherd of Hermas; The Apocalypse of Peter; The Acts of Paul, including Paul and Thecla: The Epistle of Polycarp to the Philippians; The Seven Epistles of Ignatius; The Gospel of Pseudo-Matthew; The Protevangelium of James; The Gospel of the Nativity of Mary; The Gospel of Nicodemus; The Gospel of the Saviour's Infancy; The History of Joseph the Carpenter.*

Although some of the books appeared to have value

---

*See General Biblical Introduction, H. S. Miller, 1940, Word-Bearer Press, pp. 146-149. Miller also lists some 20 books called the Pseudepigrapha, spurious and ungenuine writings that never got into the New Testament canon. Among these were "Gospels" of Andrew, Bartholomew, Barnabas, Thomas, Peter and Philip.

and were read in the churches (for example, the Shepherd of Hermas), they were excluded in the course of time, because they did not meet the required standards of genuine apostolic authorship and the teaching of correct doctrine. Much of the New Testament apocrypha contains questionable ethics, childish stories and useless miracles. As the early Christian church carefully and slowly sorted through the various writings that were claimed to be inspired, it eliminated the apocryphal books through the guidance and illumination of the Holy Spirit.

Has the canon stood the test of time?

For nearly 2000 years the Bible as we know it has been accepted by Christians as Holy Scripture. Is there adequate evidence that these books were truly "inspired by God"?

The historical accuracy and the amazing unity of the Bible's teachings have already been mentioned in Chapter 3. Archaeological discoveries of the past 200 years have shown again and again the Bible is an accurate record of historical facts. In addition hundreds of Biblical prophecies have been fulfilled and continue to be fulfilled even today—more evidence that the books chosen for the Old and New Testament canons were indeed the inspired Word of God.

The indestructability of the Bible is additional impressive evidence for its inspiration. Scripture has survived thousands of years of opposition and criticism. Indeed, history shows it has been impossible to destroy the Scriptures.

As F. F. Bruce points out, there is far more evidence for the accurate preservation of New Testament writings than for many historical manuscripts by secular writers. For example, there are but nine or ten good copies of Caesar's *Gallic War* (written between 58 B.C.

and 50 B.C.) and the oldest manuscript is 900 years later than the original. The Roman historian, Tacitus, wrote 14 volumes of his *Histories* around 100 A.D. Only four and a half volumes have survived and the oldest existing manuscripts for these are dated in the 9th and 11th centuries.

The writings of Thucydides and Herodotus, secular historians of the fifth century B.C., are known to today's scholars through existing manuscripts dated some 1200 to 1300 years after the original writings.

Existing manuscripts for the New Testament, however, date much nearer the original source and there are thousands of copies in whole or in part. The two most famous complete New Testament manuscripts are dated at around 350 A.D. One is the Codex Vaticanus, now in the Vatican Library in Rome. The other is the Codex Sinaiticus, purchased by the British from the Russians for 100,000 pounds in 1933 and now in the British Museum.

In addition to these and other complete manuscripts there are thousands of portions and fragments of New Testament writings that date from the second and third centuries A.D.

The point is this: higher critics and skeptics use ingenious methods and theories to show the unreliability and inaccuracy of Scripture. Yet, as Dr. Bruce observes, there is more evidence for the historical accuracy and correct preservation of New Testament manuscripts than there is for many writings by "... classical authors, the authenticity of which no one dreams of questioning."[*]

Today, millions of copies of the Bible roll off the presses of the world. There are portions of the Bible in more than 1,157 languages and work is underway by

[*]The New Testament Documents: Are They Reliable? F. F. Bruce, Eerdmans Publishing Co. 1943, pp. 15-17.

such groups as the Wycliffe Bible Translators to put Scripture into many other tongues.

During the turbulent times of today's Cold War and the breakdown in respect for authority and law and order, the Bible's power is still felt in all walks of life. For example, scores of athletes, amateur and professional, can testify to what Scripture has done in their lives. So can scientists, businessmen, and leaders in government. (See "For further reading" below.)

Has the Biblical canon stood the test of time? Perhaps no one could sum it up better than Martin Luther who wrote:

> Mighty potentates have raged against this Book, and sought to destroy and uproot it—Alexander the Great and princes of Egypt and Babylon, the monarchs of Persia, of Greece, and of Rome, the Emperors Julius and Augustus— but they prevailed nothing. They are gone, while the Book remains, and will remain for ever and ever, perfect and entire, as it was declared at first. Who has thus helped it— who has thus protected it against such mighty forces? No one, surely, but God Himself, who is the Master of all things...
>
> —Martin Luther

For further reading

Paperbacks

Is the Bible the Word of God? W. Graham Scroggie, Moody Press, 1922. See especially Section II, "It Claims to Be—" for useful information on the inspiration on the Old and New Testament books.

The Goal and the Glory, edited by Ted Simonson, Fleming H. Revell, 1962. Testimonies of what the Bible has done in their lives are made by 31 top athletes, including major league outfielder Felipe Alou, all-pro end Raymond Berry, and former decathelon champion Rafer Johnson.

Play Ball! James C. Hefley, Zondervan Publishing House, 1964. Sixteen personal testimonies on the Bible and Christianity by such outstanding athletes as Bill Glass, defensive end with the Cleveland Browns; Fran Tarkenton, star professional quarterback; and Bobby Richardson, former star second baseman with the New York Yankees.

Hardbacks

General Biblical Introduction, H. S. Miller, The Word-Bearer Press, 1940. See part 2: "The Canonicity of the Scriptures" chapters 12-22 for an excellent condensed summary of the Old and New Testament canon.

Can I Trust My Bible?, "What Books Belong in the Canon of Scripture?" R. Laird Harris, Moody Press, 1963. An excellent condensation of background material on the formation of Old and New Testament canons with especially interesting material on how various church fathers helped determine the apostolically genuine books of the New Testament.

The Books and the Parchments, F. F. Bruce, Fleming H. Revell, 1950. See chapter 8, "The Canon of Scripture," for more scholarly insights on how the canon was compiled from inspired authentic writings by the prophets and the apostles.

Halley's Bible Handbook, Henry H. Halley, Zondervan Publishing House, 23rd Edition, 1962. See pages 741-750 for a good capsule summary on the formation of the Old and New Testament canon.

Unger's Bible Handbook, Merrill F. Unger, Moody Press, 1966. See especially the section, "How the Bible Came to Us," pages 882-884 for useful reference material on the Old and New Testament canon.

Sports Alive! James C. Heffley, Zondervan Publishing House, 1966. Sixteen more testimonies by outstanding leaders in the athletic field who have known the life-changing power of the Bible. It includes testimonies by Bill Bradley, all-American cager at Princeton University who went on to be a Rhodes scholar at Oxford and then joined the New York Knickerbockers professional basketball team; and Paul Anderson, Olympic weight lifting champion, known as "the strongest man in the world."

CHAPTER 5

Fulfilled Bible Prophecy...
just a
Coincidence?

Just what is prophecy? And why do Christians claim that it is one of the best evidences for the inspiration of Scripture? Have very many Biblical prophecies been accurately fulfilled? Is it coincidence when Bible prophecies come true? Or is it really supernatural?

Every Christian interested in giving a reasonable answer for his faith should be familiar with fulfilled prophecy, which presents overwhelming evidence for the inspiration of Scripture.

What is prophecy?

The "prophets" in the Bible were spokesmen for God. He revealed His thoughts through the writings of these chosen men. The word "prophet" literally means "to proclaim, to declare." In one sense a prophet was a "forthteller who declared God's will to his contemporaries. But in another sense, he was a "foreteller" because his words had a predictive meaning. The prophets told —under the inspiration of the Holy Spirit—of happenings that would occur in the future.

What are marks of genuine prophecy?

Dr. S. Maxwell Coder lists at least five principles behind a genuine prophetic prediction in the Bible: Proper timing (far enough in advance); specific details (not vague generalities); freedom from ambiguity (no double meanings or misleading statements); exact fulfillment; genuine date and authorship.[*]

As mentioned in Chapter 3, Biblical higher critics of the 19th century were fond of claiming that many Bible prophecies were written hundreds of years later than originally supposed. The implication here, of course, is that such prophecies aren't prophecies at all but lies and stories concocted after so-called "predicted events" had occurred.

Archaeological discoveries have discredited these higher critical views. (See Chapter 6.) It is also well known that the Jews jealously guarded their sacred scrolls against alteration and fraud.

What are examples of fulfilled prophecies?

Striking examples of fulfilled prophecy include the fate of such magnificent ancient cities as Babylon, Tyre, and Nineveh.

Babylon was one of the greatest cities of all time. It had many modern characteristics such as an elaborate irrigation and canal system, paved streets, apartment houses, street lights, and running water. Encircling the city was a wall wide enough for driving three chariots abreast on the top. The hanging gardens of Babylon are

*The Truth Triumphant, S. Maxwell Coder and George F. Howe, Copyright 1965, Moody Bible Institute of Chicago.

well known as one of the seven wonders of the ancient world.

But because of Babylon's idolatry and because it would invade Israel and persecute God's people, God pronounced Babylon's doom through the prophet Isaiah who wrote:

> "And Babylon . . . shall be as when God overthrew Sodom and Gomorrah. It shall never be inhabited . . . neither shall the Arabian pitch tent there . . . but wild beasts of the desert shall lie there . . ." (Isaiah 13:19-21).

Isaiah wrote his prophecy around 700 B.C. One hundred years later the prophet Jeremiah predicted the imminent fall of Israel, saying that she would serve the king of Babylon 70 years (Jeremiah 25:11). Jeremiah also said:

> ". . . when seventy years are accomplished . . . I will punish the king of Babylon, and that nation . . . for their iniquity, and the land of the Chaldeans, and will make it perpetual desolations . . . and I will recompense them according to their deeds, and according to the works of their own hands" (Jeremiah 25:12-14).

Just as Isaiah had predicted, the Medes led by Cyrus attacked Babylon in 539 B.C. and destroyed most of the city. It was also later plundered by Xerxes (Cyrus' son-in-law), and Alexander the Great, who tried to restore the city but gave it up as a hopeless task.

Interestingly, Babylon's ruins created a chemical reaction in the soil, and the once fertile land was turned into an arid waste, exactly as God had predicted in Isaiah 13. By the first century A.D. Babylon was a foul-smelling, decaying ruin inhabited only by wild animals. By the twelfth century the ruins of the original city palace were impossible to reach because there were too many poisonous snakes and scorpions in the area.

The prophecy has been fulfilled even to the exact detail that " . . . neither shall the Arabian pitch tent there . . ." Dr. Cyrus Hamlin, American missionary in

Constantinople, tells of this incident:

The ruins of Babylon abound in game, and I once engaged a sheikh and his group to take me there for a week's shooting. At sundown the Arabs began to strike their tents getting ready to leave. I went to the sheikh and protested but nothing I could say had any effect. "It is not safe," he said. "No mortal flesh dare stay here after sunset. Ghosts and ghouls come out of the holes and caverns after dark, and whoever they capture becomes one of them. No Arab has ever seen the sun go down on Babylon."*

The fate of other great cities and nations has also been precisely predicted in Scripture. Tyre was a rich and prosperous seaport on the Mediterranean. Its Phoenician citizens felt secure within the "invincible" 150-foot walls. But Tyre sinned against God through pride, mistreatment of Jewish prisoners of war and breaking a treaty made with King Solomon (see Amos 1:9, 10).

In the sixth century B.C. the prophet Ezekiel predicted Tyre's doom, mentioning among other things that the city would be broken down, scraped off like a rock and that it would become a place for fishermen to spread their nets. (See Ezekiel 26:3-14, 19.) The prophecy came true, just as predicted. Nebuchadnezzar led the Medes and Persians in a 13-year siege that destroyed the mainland city. The Tyrians fled to an island a half mile off shore where Nebuchadnezzar could not follow because he had no ships. The island city lasted until 332 B.C. when Alexander the Great invaded it by tearing down the ruins of the mainland city and constructing a bridge out of the rocks and timber (a fulfillment of Ezek. 26:12, ". . . they shall lay thy stones and thy timber . . . in the midst of the water").

Tyre was destroyed violently and completely in the thirteenth century by Moslems who took it from the

*From *Christian Victory*, "Illustration Round Table," Sunday School Times Company, quoted in *The Wonder of the Word*, Gwynn McLendon Day, Moody Press, p. 52.

71

"I AM AGAINST THEE O TYRE . . . I WILL SCRAPE . . .
HER LIKE THE TOP OF A ROCK. IT SHALL BE
A PLACE FOR THE SPREADING
OF NETS IN THE MIDST OF THE SEA . . ."
(Ezekiel 26:4,5)

Crusaders. As Ezekiel promised, it has never been rebuilt and today tourists watch the fishermen spread their nets to dry on the barren rocks.

There was also the prophecy against the land of Edom, a nation of polytheists and persecutors of the Israelites (See Isaiah 34:5-12; Amos 1:11,12; Ezek. 25:14.) Edom was eventually overrun during the inter-testamental period by Jewish Maccabean forces, first in 164 B.C. and a second time in 120 B.C. After A.D. 70 when the Romans destroyed Jersualem, the Edomites disappeared and today, as Isaiah predicted, the land of Edom is a devastated ruin.

Another example is Nineveh, capital of the Assyrian empire. Although God sent Jonah in the eighth century B.C. to give the Ninevites a chance to repent of their sins, the repentance was short lived. The Assyrians were soon back to their brutal and murderous practices such as skinning prisoners of war alive. In the seventh century Nahum and Zephaniah both prophesied against Nineveh. (See Nahum 1:1-8; 2:3-6; 3:7. Also Zephaniah

2:13-15.) Nineveh was destroyed in 612 B.C. when Babylonian and Median forces diverted the Tigris River and caused a flood to literally dissolve the buildings and walls as predicted in Nahum 2:6.

Biblical higher critics denied the existence of Nineveh for many years and only in the nineteenth century did archaeologists finally dig up evidence of its existence. Ironically, because Nineveh disappeared without a trace, critics of the Bible who claimed Nineveh was not even there only underscored Nahum's prophecy: "Nineveh is laid waste: who will bemoan her?" (Nahum 3:7).*

What are some fulfilled prophecies concerning Jesus Christ—the Messiah?

There are some 333 Old Testament predictions concerning the Messiah, which are fulfilled by Jesus Christ in the New Testament. Messianic prophecy begins with Genesis 3:15:

"And I will put enmity between thee and the woman, and between thy seed and her seed; it shall bruise thy head, and thou shalt bruise his heel."

This prophecy, uttered against Satan himself, predicted that the Messiah would someday deal Satan a fatal blow, while receiving a serious but not totally fatal wound Himself. This of course is exactly what happened when Christ died on the cross (the "bruising of His heel") but then rose from the grave to conquer death and guarantee Satan's eventual fate (the "bruising of his head").

On p. 75 is a partial list of additional Messianic prophecies from the Old Testament and how Jesus Christ fulfilled them in the New Testament.

*For more information, see series on "Prophecy" by Herbert H. Ehrenstein in Eternity magazine, September and October issues, 1966. Also see Chapter 3, "The Proof of Prophecy," in The Wonder of the Word, Gwynn McLendon Day, Moody Press, 1957.

Jesus was also a prophet. He made many predictions that were fulfilled including announcement of his own crucifixion three years before it happened (John 3:14). He also declared His resurrection three years ahead of time (John 2:19,21). He predicted the complete destruction of the Jewish temple in Jerusalem (Matt. 24:2). And this occurred as predicted in A.D. 70 when the Roman forces under Titus destroyed Jerusalem and the temple.

What about fulfilled prophecies concerning Israel?

Much in the news in the last two decades, the nation of Israel has provided the world with the opportunity to watch Bible prophecy fulfilled before its eyes. Two of the most obvious predictions and their fulfillments concerning Israel deal with: 1) the predicted dispersion of the Jews and their return to their native land; 2) the prediction of a complete transformation in Israel.

In Deuteronomy 28:64-68 Moses prophesied the scattering of the Jews:

"And the Lord shall scatter thee among all people, from the one end of the earth even unto the other . . . And among these nations shalt thou find no ease, neither shall the sole of thy foot have rest: but the Lord shall give thee there a trembling heart . . . and sorrow of mind: And thy life shall hang in doubt before thee . . . and thou shalt have none assurance of thy life . . . And the Lord shall bring thee into Egypt again with ships . . . and there ye shall be sold unto your enemies . . ."

Fifteen centuries passed before this prophecy was fulfilled. In A.D. 70 Titus the Roman general led his forces in destruction of Jerusalem. All surviving captives over age 17 were sent to Egypt (by ships) to work in the mines. From that day until the mid-twentieth century the Jews were a scattered persecuted people. Today, however, you can see the fulfillment of other Bible prophecy concerning Israel. Isaiah and Jeremiah both predicted that the Jews would not always be

74

Examples of how Christ fulfilled prophecy

Messianic Prophecy

"But thou, Bethlehem Ephrata, though thou be little among the thousands of Judah, yet out of thee shall he come forth unto me that is to be ruler in Israel; whose goings forth have been from of old, from everlasting" (Micah 5:2, 700 B.C.).

"Rejoice greatly, O daughter of Zion; shout, O daughter of Jerusalem: behold, thy king cometh unto thee: he is just, and having salvation; lowly, and riding upon an ass, and upon a colt the foal of an ass" (Zechariah 9:9, 500 B.C.).

"I gave my back to the smiters and my cheeks to them that plucked off the hair: I hid not my face from shame and spitting" (Isaiah 50:6, 700 B.C.).

". . . And he was numbered with the transgressors; and he bare the sin of many, and made intercession for the transgressors" (Isaiah 53:12, 700 B.C.).

"They part my garments among them, and cast lots upon my vesture" (Psalm 22:18, 1000 B.C.).

"He keepeth all his bones; not one of them is broken" (Psalm 34:20, 1000 B.C.).

"For thou wilt not leave my soul in hell; neither wilt thou suffer thine Holy One to see corruption" (Psalm 16:10, 1000 B.C.).

Fulfillment in Christ

"Now when Jesus was born in Bethlehem of Judea in the days of Herod the king . . ." (Matt. 2:1, also see John 8:58 ". . . Before Abraham was, I am").

"And the disciples went, and did as Jesus commanded them, and brought the ass, and the colt, and put on them their clothes, and they set him thereon . . . And the multitudes that went before, and that followed, cried, saying, Hosanna to the son of David: Blessed is he that cometh in the name of the Lord . . ." (Matt. 21:6, 7, 9).

"Then did they spit in his face and buffeted him; and others smote him with the palms of their hands" (Matt. 26:67).

"And with him they crucify two thieves; the one on his right hand, and the other on his left" (Mark 15:27); "then said Jesus, Father, forgive them; for they know not what they do . . ." (Luke 23:34).

"Then the soldiers, when they had crucified Jesus, took his garments and made four parts . . . now the coat was without seam, woven from the top throughout. They said therefore among themselves, Let us not rend it, but cast lots for it, whose it shall be . . ." (John 19:23, 24).

"But when they came to Jesus, and saw that he was dead already, they brake not his legs . . . (John 19:33).

"And the angel answered and said unto the women, Fear not ye; for I know that ye seek Jesus, which was crucified. He is not here: for he is risen, as he said . . ." (Matt. 28:5, 6).

scattered but that they would return to their Holy
Land:

"Fear not: for I am with thee: I will bring thy seed from
the east, and gather thee from the west: . . . bring my sons
from far, and my daughters from the ends of the earth"
(Isaiah 43:5, 6).

". . . I will gather you from all the nations, and from all
the places whither I have driven you, saith the Lord; and I
will bring you again into the place whence I caused you to
be carried away captive" (Jeremiah 29:14).

Over 1800 years passed before the Jews began their
return. During the latter part of the nineteenth century
the Moslems, who had occupied Palestine since the
sixth century A.D., revoked a law forbidding Jews to
own land in the country. By the turn of the century,
Zionism (Jewish nationalism) was a full-fledged move-
ment under the brilliant leadership of Theodor Herzl.
By 1914 some 90,000 Jews were living in Palestine in
43 agricultural settlements. In 1917 the British issued
the Balfour Declaration, favoring establishment in
Palestine of a national home for the Jews. In 1922 the
Council of the League of Nations approved a mandate
over Palestine to be held by Great Britain.

More Jews continued to flow into the land much to
the distress of the Arab (Moslem) inhabitants who made
up a majority of the population. By 1935 there were
300,000 Jews in Palestine and by 1936 Jews actually
owned by purchase 350,000 acres of land which they
used mostly for agricultural purposes.

Despite Arab protests the Jewish state of Israel was
established in 1948. The United States recognized Israel as a nation immediately and Russia soon followed.
On May 11, 1949, Israel was accepted by the United
Nations by a vote of 37 to 12.*

*This brief synopsis of the rise of modern Israel is based on Israeli/
Arab Conflict and the Bible, Wilbur M. Smith, G/L Regal Books,
1967, pp. 61-73.

Not only have the Jews returned to their homeland as prophesied. Other Old Testament prophesies promising the restoration of the destroyed land of Palestine are also being fulfilled before the eyes of today's world. Isaiah and Ezekiel predicted this restoration over 2500 years ago:

"For the Lord sall comfort Zion: he will comfort all her waste places: and he will make her wilderness like Eden, and her desert like the garden of the Lord" (Isaiah 51:3).

"And they shall build the old wastes, they shall raise up the former desolations, and they shall repair the waste cities, the desolations of many generations" (Isaiah 61:4).

"And the desolate land shall be tilled, whereas it lay desolate in the sight of all that passed by. And they shall say, This land that was desolate is become like the garden of Eden . . ." (Ezekiel 36:34, 35).

Today, the visitor to Israel is overwhelmed by the transformation of the land that—before the establishment of the new Israeli nation—consisted mostly of barren desert and malarial swamps. In a few short years the tiny nation of Israel has erected modern cities, with skyscrapers and rapid transit systems. There are thriving industries and fertile fields. Through conservation and irrigation the Jewish people have turned the desert into fruitful fields and orchards and Palestine can now truly be called a garden spot of the world.

Israel has also developed technologically (including nuclear reactors), and Israeli technicians are helping give aid to 65 countries. Israel's military prowess is also well-known through her victories over the surrounding Arab nations in 1948 and 1967.

Modern Israel and the Jews themselves are living proof of literal fulfillment of the inspired prophetic Word of God—the Bible.*

*For additional sources of information on Israel, see "For Further Reading," p. 80.

What are the chances against fulfilled prophecy "just happening"?

Peter W. Stoner, scientist and mathematician, worked with over 600 college students over several years applying the "principle of probability" to Bible prophecy. (This principle holds that if the chance of one thing happening is one in M and the chance of another thing happening is one in N, then the chance that they shall both happen is one in M times N.) In a chapter titled "Prophetic Accuracy" in his book, *Science Speaks*, Stoner points out that such theories of probability as one in M times N are the basis for fixing all types of insurance rates. The accuracy of the principle of probability has been proved in practical experience again and again.*

Stoner asked the 600 college students with whom he worked to be "very conservative in fixing their estimates" as they applied the one in M times N principle to Bible prophecy. Stoner does not claim that the students' estimates are necessarily infallible and he admits that some estimates may be too small and others may be too large. He invites anyone who wishes to use the principle to make his own estimates, which he is sure will still turn out to be "very conclusive" in showing that fulfillment of Bible prophecy is extremely difficult to explain as "coincidence."

Stoner gives an example of how his students applied the principle of probability to the prophecy of the destruction of Tyre and the seven definite events that were supposed to take place: 1) Nebuchadnezzar shall take the city of Tyre; 2) Other nations would help fulfill

*See **Science Speaks**, Peter W. Stoner, copyright 1958, Moody Bible Institute, p. 70. Dr. Stoner was chairman of the departments of mathematics, astronomy and engineering at Pasadena (Calif.) City College and also served as Chairman of the natural science division at Westmont College, Santa Barbara, Calif. He is a charter member of the American Scientific Affiliation.

the prophecy; 3) Tyre would be made flat like the top of a rock; 4) Tyre would become a place for spreading of nets; 5) Tyre's stones and timber would be laid in the sea; 6) Other cities would have great fear because of the fall of Tyre; 7) The old city of Tyre would never be rebuilt.

Stoner's students estimated the chances of the occurrence of the seven events as follows: No. 1—one in two; No. 2—one in five; No. 3—one in 2000; No. 4—one in ten; No. 5—one in ten; No. 6—one in ten; No. 7—one in twenty. By multiplying all of these estimates together the students came up with the final equation: 1 in 2x5x2000x10x10x10x20 or 1 in 400 million.

Similar estimates were made concerning many other Bible prophecies including the destruction of Babylon. Again seven specific events were predicted, such as the destruction of Babylon, that it would never again be inhabited, Arabs would not pitch their tents there, men would not pass by the ruins, etc. The students estimated these events and came out with a final answer of one in 100 billion.

Stoner and his students also applied the principle of probability to eight prophecies concerning Jesus Christ: Micah 5:2; Malachi 3:1; Zechariah 9:9; Zechariah 13:6; Zechariah 11:12; Zechariah 11:13; Isaiah 53:7; Psalm 22:16. When the estimates were multiplied together the final chance of all eight of these prophecies being fulfilled in one man were totaled at one in 10^{32} (one in 100,000,000,000,000,000,000,000,000,000,000).

Let it be reemphasized that—as Stoner himself admits—the first estimates of probability on a prophecy can change according to a person's personal opinions. However, what Stoner's computations do show is that when one starts applying the principle of probability to any series of events, the chances of having these events occur exactly as predicted become astronomically large.

For example, suppose you would predict it would rain tomorrow. You would have one chance in two of being right. But suppose you also predict that in addition to the rain the weather would turn warmer. Your chances now jump to one in four of being right. The odds build as you predict more elements. For example, if you predict four distinct elements you would have one chance in sixteen of being correct. If you make ninety specific predictions your chances of being correct in all ninety instances are one in an octillion.

The skeptic can call fulfilled Bible prophecy coincidence or mere chance if he wishes, but even by the most conservative estimates the "odds are against him."

Fulfilled prophecy does not "prove" the divine inspiration of Scripture. But fulfilled prophecy does provide undeniable evidence that the Bible is a supernatural book, written with more than human knowledge.

The Christian sees the hand of God in fulfilled prophecy. It is as if the entire world is a stage; God pre-wrote the drama of human history and then left men free to act it out, yet always within His divine will.

For further reading

Paperbacks

Israeli-Arab Conflict and the Bible, Wilbur M. Smith, G/L Regal Books, 1967. Contains 162 pages by one of today's outstanding authorities on the Bible and the Holy Land. Written only weeks after the Israeli-Arab clash in June, 1967, this book discusses the prophetic significance of Israel's return to Palestine and the possession of the entir? city of Jerusalem for the first time since 587 B.C.

The Wonder of the Word, Gwynn McLendon Day, Moody Press, 1957. See Chapter 3, "Proof of Prophecy."

Hardbacks

The Bible, Science and Creation, S. Maxwell Coder and George F. Howe, Moody Press, 1965. See Chapter 11, "The Bible and Prophecy."

Protestant Christian Evidences, Bernard Ramm, Moody Press, 1954. See Chapter 3, "Supernatural Verification Through Fulfilled Prophecy" for an excellent explanation of what prophecy means and why it is undeniable evidence for the supernatural inspiration of the Bible.

Periodicals

Five part series on "prophecy" by Herbert H. Ehrenstein, *Eternity* magazine, August-December 1966. Extremely readable material on the place and meaning of Bible prophecy, examples of specifically fulfilled prophecies concerning ancient nations and cities, the coming of the Messiah in Jesus Christ, the Church in the last days.

"The Amazing Rise of Israel!" John F. Walvoord, *Moody Monthly,* October 1967. Also see in this same special issue on the Bible and prophecy: "Why Did God Choose Israel?", "The Pieces Fall Together," and "God in History."

"Israel—Land of Promise," John Scofield and B. Anthony Stewart, *National Geographic,* March 1965. Excellent text and photographs that graphically illustrate how Israel is fulfilling Biblical prophecies today.

See also the December 1967 issue of *Holiday* magazine which was dedicated entirely to Israel, her history, her heritage and her phenomenal development in the twentieth century.

CHAPTER 6

Archaeology...
friend or foe of
the Bible?

Archaeology is a science that has developed during the last 200 years. Interestingly enough, the first archaeological discoveries were being made when liberal higher criticism of the Bible was becoming popular. Those who placed their faith "in the assured results of higher criticism" looked confidently to the results of archaeological expeditions to confirm charges that the Bible was inaccurate, full of errors and untrustworthy as an historical document. Archaeology, however, has proved to be no friend of higher criticism. The objective results of spade and shovel show an overwhelming accumulation of evidence that supports the Bible.

What is archaeology?

Archaeology is the "science of ancient things." General archaeology deals with the excavation, decipherment and critical evaluation of records from the ancient past. Biblical archaeology is a more specialized field that focuses on ancient records of the past that touch directly or indirectly upon the Bible and its message.*

Precision and care go into every phase of an archaeological "dig," from selection of the site, which is done with surveying instruments, to the digging itself and the recording of findings and the final report. Because archaeology is basically destruction (as buildings, walls, etc., are uncovered, they are dismantled piece by piece), detailed records are kept on every step of the operation. Frail objects made of wood and bone are often chemically treated for preservative purposes. As an excavation proceeds, workers accumulate sketches, surveyor's plans and numerous objects in pottery, wood, stone, bone, etc.**

Of what practical value is Biblical archaeology?

Archaeology confirms the Bible and shows that its historical statements are true and accurate. Secondly, archaeology illustrates and illuminates the Bible and sheds new light on Bible texts to help explain their meaning.

It is archaeology's amazing confirmation of Scripture that is of particular significance to the Christian. In the nineteenth century liberal higher criticism and evolutionism (substitution of Darwin's theory on organic evolution for God) joined together to attempt to literally "tear the Bible apart." Until various Biblical sites were uncovered by archaeologists, liberal critics of Scripture had a field day as they busily dissected Bible manuscripts by means of assumptions, guesses, and wild theories that they could not really substantiate. Christians who held to a conservative view of the Bible as trustworthy history were often branded as ignorant and hopelessly behind the times.

*Unger's Bible Dictionary, Merrill F. Unger, Copyright 1957, Moody Bible Institute, p. 78.
**The Biblical World, edited by Charles F. Pfeiffer, Baker Book House, 1966, p. 60, 61.

Archaeology, however, has proved to be the friend not the foe of conservative Christianity. Time and time again in the nineteenth and twentieth centuries the "very stones have cried out" (Luke 19:40) to testify to the Bible's historical accuracy.

Dr. W. F. Albright, recognized as this century's foremost Palestinian archaeologist, has admitted that there can be little doubt that archaeology has confirmed the substantial historicity of Old Testament tradition.[*] Nelson Glueck, famed Jewish archaeologist, has stated that no archaeological discovery has ever contradicted or voided a Biblical reference.[**] Millar Burrows, Yale University, has declared that archaeology has " ... unquestionably strengthened confidence in the reliability of the Scriptural record..." and that "... in many cases it has refuted the views of modern critics."[***]

What are some examples of how archaeology has refuted critics of the Bible?

Examples of how archaeology has completely refuted the claims of liberal higher critics of the Bible include:

Verification of King Solomon's wealth and greatness. Higher critics doubted the truth of Biblical accounts in I Kings, which described the grandeur of King Solomon. The Bible mentions that Solomon had a navy (I Kings 9:26). His wealth was supposed to be staggering, for example, he had a vast number of horses and chariots (I Kings 10:26). He was also, according to Scripture, a great builder who had access to metal refinery equipment. For a description of how brass (bronze) was used when building the Temple, see I Kings 7, 8.

Archaelogical discoveries of this century provide conclusive evidence that Solomon was indeed as great a king as Scripture describes. Excavations led by Dr. Henry Breasted at Megiddo in northern Palestine between 1925-34

[*]Archaeology and the Religion of Israel, W. F. Albright, Copyright 1956, Johns Hopkins Press.
[**]Rivers in the Desert, Nelson Glueck, Copyright 1959, the Jewish Publication Society of America, p. 31.
[***]What Mean These Stones? Millar Burrows. Copyright 1941. American Schools of Royal Research, pp. 291-292.

revealed one of Solomon's "chariot cities." Among other finds were stables capable of holding over 400 horses. Stalls arranged in double rows were uncovered, including stone mangers and massive stone hitching posts. Other buildings in the vicinity revealed barracks for Solomon's chariot battalions, which were stationed at the strategic site of Megiddo. Their job was to guard the pass that was part of the main commercial and military highway from Egypt to Syria.

Another find that substantiates Solomon's greatness is the seaport town of Ezion-geber on the shore of the Red Sea. Nelson Glueck, director of the American Schools of Oriental Research, led excavations here in 1938-40 that revealed a large and highly developed factory for the refining of copper and iron. Here was source of the metal that Solomon's trading ships used when bartering for gold, silver and ivory (I Kings 9:28, 10:22). Here, too, was where the brass was made for the temple at Jerusalem.

The existence of King Sargon (mentioned only once in Scripture in Isaiah 20:1) was doubted by Bible critics for many years. They speculated for the benefit of "backward conservatives" that the name of Sargon was invented by a Biblical writer to fill in some chronological gap. Excavations in Mesopotamia in the mid-nineteenth century by Englishman Austen Layard and Frenchman Paul Emile Botta uncovered King Sargon's palace, parts of which are on display today at the Oriental Institute at the University of Chicago. One such piece is a large stone bull, weighing 40 tons—rather weighty evidence that the supposedly non-existent King Sargon did reign at one time as King in Assyria.

Existence of the Hittites was also doubted by higher critics of the nineteenth century. The Bible mentions the Hittites some 40 times, for example, Joshua 1:4. According to Scripture, the Hittites were big and important enough to cause the Syrians to flee from Israel (II Kings 7:6). But there was no reference to the Hittites in the fragmentary pagan literature available to critics of a century ago. Therefore, with true rationalistic logic, higher critics deduced that the Hittites never existed.

Later in the nineteenth century archaeologist A. H. Sayce identified certain inscriptions discovered in Syria as Hittite. In 1906 Hugh Winckler excavated the Hittite capital of Boghazkoy, recovering thousands of Hittite texts including the Hittite code.*

*"The Bible's Critics Use a Double Standard," Edwin M. Yamauchi, *Christianity Today*, November 19, 1965, p. 4.

Substantiation of the remarkable prophecies in the Book of Daniel is also credited to archaeology.

One of the chief criticisms of Daniel was the mention of King Belshazzar in the fifth chapter. According to Daniel, Belshazzar was killed on the night that the Medes and Persians captured Babylon. Secular historians, however, never mentioned Belshazzar and stated that the last king of Babylon was Nabonidus, who was supposedly not present when the city was captured and was later captured by the Medes and Persians. Critics chortled over this "clear case of error" in the Bible and in characteristic fashion chose to believe secular historians rather than the Word of God.

The two accounts remained in seeming conflict until 1853, when Sir Henry Rawlinson dug up a cylinder in the Euphrates Valley with an inscription that reported there were two kings of Babylon during Daniel's lifetime, a father and his son. Nabonidus had made his son Belshazzar co-ruler of Babylon. Because Nabonidus was absent when the Persians attacked his life was spared, but his son Belshazzar, co-regent of Babylon, died in the battle. This co-regency by father and son helps explain Daniel 5:7 when Daniel is described as being made "the third ruler" in the kingdom.

The preceding examples are only a handful of the scores of archaeological discoveries that have substantiated the Bible and refuted higher criticism. *Unger's Bible Handbook* records almost 100 such discoveries (see "For Further Reading," p. 91) and new finds are being made constantly.

The Pool of Bethesda (where Jesus healed a lame man, John 5:2-15) has been discovered in the northeast corner of the old city of Jerusalem.*

In June 1961 an Italian archaeological expedition excavated ancient Caesarea and found fresh evidence that Pontius Pilate was indeed the high commissioner of Judea between A.D. 26 and A.D. 36.

Also uncovered in 1961 was the ancient south wall of the original Jerusalem, built by the Jebusites. This

*See **The New Testament Documents, Are They Reliable?** F. F. Bruce, Eerdmans, 1943, p. 94. According to Dr. Bruce "few sites in Jerusalem, mentioned in the Gospels, can be identified so confidently."

Jebusite fort was the one captured by David's men under Joab (I Chron. 11:6) and was renamed the City of David (II Sam. 5:9).*

Among those who have done extensive digging in Jerusalem since 1961 is Dr. Kathleen Kenyon, world's foremost woman archaeologist. Dr. Kenyon, famed excavator of Jericho between 1952 and 1958 (see *Digging Up Jericho*, Frederick A. Praeger Publisher, 1957) has concentrated on helping establish the original boundaries of pre-Israelite Jerusalem.** Her findings include new data on the Spring Gihon, ancient Jerusalem's water supply, which King Hezekiah connected with the Pool of Siloam by means of a tunnel in 710 B.C. (see II Kings 20:20).

Also of great significance to Bible scholars (and unquestionably the most publicized) have been the discoveries of the Dead Sea Scrolls (1947-1956) and the 1963-65 excavations at Masada, one time fortress and winter palace of Herod the Great (see Matt. 2:1).

What are the Dead Sea Scrolls and why are they important?

Hailed as the most significant archaeological find in this century, the Dead Sea Scrolls are manuscripts discovered in caves on the northwestern corner of the Dead Sea between 1947 and 1956. The scrolls were written during a period between 200 B.C. and A.D. 50 by sectarian Jews known as Essenes who lived in a community now known by the Arabic name of Qumran.

The scrolls include some 500 to 600 manuscripts, many of which are books of the Old Testament. The reason that the scrolls are considered so valuable and significant is that before their discovery the oldest known manuscript of the Hebrew Old Testament was

*See "When the Stones Speak," Decision, February, 1962.
**As reported in the Jerusalem Post Weekly, Sept. 18, 1967.

dated at A.D. 826. The Dead Sea Scrolls provide portions of the Old Testament in Hebrew that date back to 150 B.C., possibly 200 B.C. This means that Christians now possess manuscripts that are 1,000 years nearer the original Old Testament writings.

Comparison of the Dead Sea Scroll Old Testament manuscripts with the Masoretic Hebrew text of A.D. 826 shows that they are substantially the same. Dr. William S. LaSor, Hebrew scholar who has done much research on the scrolls, observes that "... there is no significant difference that alters any essential item of our Christian faith."[*]

The Dead Sea Scrolls include parts or fragments of every book of the Old Testament except Esther. There are large portions of Samuel and Habakkuk and one complete copy of the Book of Isaiah.

Only 30 miles south of the caves that hid the Dead Sea Scrolls is Masada, site of an ancient fortress built on a huge rock towering some 1300 feet above the western shore of the Dead Sea. Excavated from 1963-65 by large numbers of volunteers working with no pay under direction of Israeli archaeologist and military leader Yigael Yadin, Masada has yielded one of the most exciting and intriguing stories ever uncovered by archaeology.

Masada was once the winter palace and reserve fortress refuge of Herod the Great (king of Judea at the birth of Christ, Matt. 2:1). The fortress was occupied by Jewish Zealots in A.D. 66 at the start of the revolt against Rome that led to the destruction of Jerusalem by Titus and his legions in A.D. 70. The Jewish patriots held out at Masada until A.D. 73, but the 960 inhabi-

---

[*]"The Dead Sea Scrolls After Twenty Years," Dr. William Sanford LaSor, The Sunday School Times and Gospel Herald, August 1, 1967, p. 9.

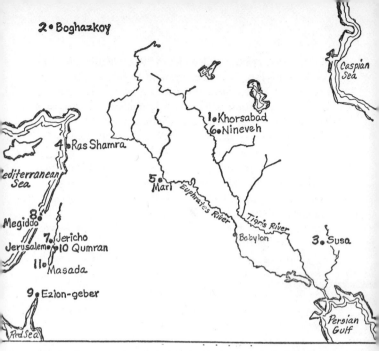

Outstanding examples of the hundreds of archaeological finds of great significance and interest are numbered on the map above. Included are the following, with the dates of each discovery:

(1) Discovery of Sargon's palace at Khorsabad (1843) rescued King Sargon from supposed "non-existence."

(2) Hittite Monuments at Boghazkoy (1906) provided extensive evidence that the Hittites did exist.

(3) The Code of Hammurabi, uncovered at Susa (1901) was the first important legal document showing the use of Mosaic laws.

(4) The Ras Shamra Tablets (1927-1937) furnish historical authentication of the debauched nature of Canaanite Baal worship.

(5) The Mari Letters (1935-1938) resurrected the brilliant history of the famous city state of Mari on the Middle Euphrates River and shed light on the legal and social customs of Biblical patriarchs such as Abraham, Isaac and Jacob.

(6) Nineveh, site of discovery (1853) of the wonderful library collected in the seventh century B.C. by King Ashurbanipal who sent scribes far and wide to collect copies of early writings.

(7) Jericho, where excavations by Kathleen Kenyon (1952-58) reveal some of the oldest "town" ruins ever uncovered.

(8) Megiddo, site of extensive finds (1925-34) including stables where Solomon quartered over 400 horses.

(9) Ezion-geber, Solomon's 10th century B.C. metal refinery discovered by archaeologist Nelson Glueck (1938-40). Glueck says the refinery and the mines made Solomon a copper magnate.

(10) The Dead Sea Scrolls discovered (1947) in a cave at Qumran near the Dead Sea, provide us with the oldest known Old Testament manuscripts.

(11) Masada, mountain stronghold and fortress of King Herod the Great, where recent excavations by archaeologist Yigael Yadin (1963-65) revealed the dramatic story of Masada's final siege, as well as additional documents similar to the Dead Sea Scrolls.

tants, men, women and children, were finally besieged by thousands of Roman troops and faced certain defeat. Rather than surrender themselves to slavery, the defenders of Masada killed their families and themselves in gallant defiance of Roman oppression.*

Masada's secrets are significant to Bible scholarship for several reasons. Not only do they throw further light on Herod the Great, contemporary of Christ, but fragments of Biblical writings similar to the Dead Sea Scrolls have been found there. In addition, the excavations of Masada have substantiated to practically the last detail the report of first century historian Flavius Josephus, only source of historical information on Masada. This same Josephus is one of the main sources of historical reference to Christ found outside the Bible. (See Chapter 2.)

Does archaeology provide "final proof" of the inspiration and authority of the Bible?

The Bible, of course, does not need "final proof." The authority of Scripture does not rest on the ability of Christians to prove it is true. God's revelation is given to man to be believed.

Christianity, however, is a faith that rests on facts (actual events), and it is important that these facts can be verified. An unbelievable fact would be a contradiction in terms. Archaeology provides increasing evidence that the facts of the Bible are trustworthy and believable, not just myths and stories.

While the Christian does not base his trust in Christ on the number of archaeological arguments he can offer

---

*For an excellent account of the Masada expedition see Masada: Herod's Fortress and the Zealot's Last Stand, Yigael Yadin, Random House, 1966. Yadin, professor of archaeology at Hebrew University in Jerusalem, served as Chief of Operations of the Israel Defence Forces during the Israeli War of Liberation in 1948. In addition to the Masada excavation, Yadin has done much research on the Dead Sea Scrolls.

in favor of Scripture, he does find tremendous use for archaeological evidence. As archaeological scholar Howard Vos points out, the Christian who knows something about archaeology has a valuable ally in the secular and agnostic classroom, where attacks on orthodox Christianity can be made with skillful disdain.

Archaeological discoveries are also valuable for helping the Christian discern fact from non-Christian opinion as he reads today's literature, textbooks, newspapers and popular magazines.

As Vos suggests, every Christian should be acquainted with the findings of archaeology and make these facts an effective weapon for not only defending Scripture but for sharing the meaning of faith in Christ with others who seek to know.[*]

[*]See An Introduction to Bible Archaeology, Howard F. Vos, Moody Press, 1956, p. 125.

For further study

Paperbacks

An Introduction to Bible Archaeology, Howard F. Vos, Moody Press, 1956, 127 pages. Contains good bibliography and gives good basic introduction to the purposes of archaeology, how archaeologists work, and how archaeology has shed much light on the Biblical records.

Genesis and Archaeology, Howard F. Vos, Moody Press, 1963, 127 pages. Contains useful information on the Creation, the fall of man, the Flood, Abraham and other patriarchs.

Dead Sea Scrolls and the Christian Faith, William Sanford LaSor, Moody Press, 1956, 251 pages. A thorough but not exhausting study of the Dead Sea Scrolls for the layman from a scholarly but informative viewpoint.

Hardbacks

The Bible, Science and Creation, S. Maxwell Coder, and George F. Howe, Moody Press, 1965. See Chapters 9 and 10 on "The Bible and Archaeology."

Unger's Bible Handbook, Merrill F. Unger, Moody Press, 1966. See pages 18-33 for 94 archaeological discoveries related to specific Bible references. Other archaeological material appears in many chapters.

Halley's Bible Handbook, Henry H. Halley, Zondervan Publishing House, 1962. See pages 42-57 for important archaeological discoveries that refute higher criticism and substantiate Biblical historical accounts.

The Biblical World, A Dictionary of Biblical Archaeology, edited by Charles F. Pfeiffer, Baker Book House, 1966, 612 pages. A well-illustrated reference book covering hundreds of subjects. Contributors include the best of conservative scholarship in the area of archaeology and other Biblical studies.

Masada, Yigael Yadin, Random House, 1966. The fascinating story of King Herod's fortress-palace on the shores of the Dead Sea, where 960 Jewish patriots made a gallant last stand against Roman legions in A.D. 73, and where unpaid volunteers from throughout the world made thrilling archaeological discoveries almost 1900 years later.

CHAPTER 7

Are there myths in the Bible?

The scene is a secular college classroom. The subject is "Classical Mythology." The professor is saying: "And so, in examining the three great myths of creation we find noted similarities between the Sumerian account, the Babylonian account and the Hebrew account found in the first chapter of Genesis."

And from there the professor goes on to make precise comparisons linking the polytheism of the Babylonians to the monotheism of the Bible and Christianity.

Is there an answer for the secular non-Christian approach that equates Biblical accounts such as the creation of the earth in Genesis 1 with pagan myths? This chapter will explore the basic question, "Who says there are myths in Scripture?" by examining the evidence. Christians have nothing to fear from the truth.

93

What they must guard against are not myths *in* the Bible, but myths people tell *about* the Bible.

What is the difference between monotheism and pagan polytheism?

Basic understanding of the difference between monotheism and polytheism is absolutely necessary to help the Christian examine the charge that such myths as the Babylonian creation account are similar to Genesis 1, and therefore Genesis 1 is myth,* too.

Anthropologists are disagreed on what came first, monotheism or polytheism. Those who essentially hold an evolutionistic position say that man started with polytheism because he evolved from a common primate ancestor with the anthropoid apes. According to this position man made an ascent from apish chatter and fear of the dark unknown to animatism, which means he believed in a terrifying, unscrutable force.

Next came animism, which is similar to the religion of many isolated tribes who fear evil spirits. Next was polytheism, which was immortalized in the Greek myths. The contribution of the Hebrews was that they were able to move from polytheism to a concept of one tribal god, then later to full grown monotheism.**

According to the Bible, however, the first man was a monotheist—that is, he worshiped one God. Not all anthropologists are evolutionists and many scholars agree with the Biblical view that early man was mon-

---

*According to Webster, a "myth" is a parable or allegory, something having only an imaginary or unverifiable existence. Higher critics of Scripture claim that many of the accounts in the Bible, such as creation, the Flood, or the resurrection are stories that Jews and Christians came to believe were true, but which were not based on fact. Rudolph Bultmann, existentialist theologian, is well known for his "demythologizing of Scripture," meaning that he discounts the miraculous elements in the Bible and seeks to find the "theological truth" behind what he thinks are "mythical stories."

See **Religion: Origins and Ideas, Robert Grow. Inter-Varsity Fellowship, 1966, p. 10.

otheistic and that he later turned to idolatry and worship of self-made gods.*

The Bible is a graphic record of how man turned from the worship of one true God to idolatry. The Jewish prophets of the Old Testament were continually warning the people against worshiping idols, but the Israelites constantly fell into idolatry because they failed to give God their complete allegiance. (See for example Exod. 32:4, Num. 25:2, I Kings 11:5. For a graphic summary of man's turning away from God see Paul's account in Rom. 1:18-31.)

What pagan myths have been found to be similar to Bible accounts?

Archaeological evidence has been uncovered in the form of seven clay tablets giving mythical accounts of creation, the fall and the flood. Most famous of the archaeological sites that yielded such tablets is the library of Ashurbanipal, which was excavated at Nineveh, ancient capital of the Assyrian Empire, by Austen H. Layard, Hormuzd Rassam and George Smith from 1848 to 1876.

Ashurbanipal (668 to 626 B.C.) was an Assyrian king with a deep interest in learning and scholarship. He amassed a library of thousands of clay tablets by sending scribes throughout Mesopotamia to copy and, if necessary, translate the existing literature of his day. Found among these tablets was the Babylonian creation account known as the "Enuma Elish," which dates to the days of Hammurabi, King of Babylonia around 1700 B.C.**

---

*Scholars holding a position of monotheism degenerating into polytheism include William Schmidt, Steven Langdon, and well-known archaeologist, Sir William M. Petrie, who discovered evidence that the first religion of the Egyptians was a form of monotheism.
**Genesis and Archaeology, Howard F. Vos, Moody Press, 1963, p. 12.

Also discovered in King Ashurbanipal's library in Nineveh was an ancient Babylonian legend called the "Myth of Adapa," which parallels the fall of man in Genesis 3. The third famous find from Ashurbanipal's library is a Babylonian version of the flood known as the "Epic of Gilgamesh."

What is the "plot" of the Babylonian creation myth?

The Enuma Elish (Babylonian creation myth) is told on seven clay tablets. Tablet one describes the opening scene, a primitive age when only "uncreated world matter" existed. This "uncreated matter" was personified by two mythical beings: Apsu, the male, who represented the primeval fresh water ocean, and Tiamat, the female, who represented the primeval salt water ocean. This mythical pair become the parents of a host of other gods that appear as the Babylonian account progresses.

In tablets two and three, the offspring of Apsu and Tiamat become so annoying that Apsu decides to do away with them all. But Apsu's plan is discovered by the great god, Ea. Ea kills Apsu and then begets Marduk, city god of Babylon, and main hero of the myth.

Tablet four describes Marduk's elevation to supremacy over all the gods of Babylon. Meanwhile, Tiamat is creating an "army" of monsters to avenge the death of her husband, Apsu. She names a god called Kingu as commander-in-chief of her new forces.

Marduk and Tiamat have a showdown and Marduk kills Tiamat with an arrow that pierces her heart. Marduk then slices Tiamat in two and from half of her body creates the sky and the heavens and from the other half he creates the earth.

Tablet five tells how Marduk appoints the moon to rule over the night and to mark the days and months of

"HIGHLIGHTS" OF THE BABYLONIAN MYTH

"Highlights" of the Babylonian creation myth include a battle between the female god, Tiamat, and the Babylonian city god, Marduk, who kills Tiamat (1), splits her in two (2) and uses one half to make the sky (3), the other half as a foundation for the earth (4). The text of the myth reads: "Tiamat and Marduk, the wisest of the gods, took their stands opposite each other. They pressed to battle and drew near in combat. He shot off an arrow, it tore her belly, it cut through her vitals, it pierced [her] heart. He split her open like a mussel into two parts; half of her he set in place and formed the sky . . . and a great structure, its counterpart, he established Esharra (the earth) . . ."

Tablet VI of the myth tells how Kingu, commander of Tiamat's army, is slain (5). Marduk instructs his father, the god, Ea, to use Kingu's blood (6) to create man (7), who is to be servant to the gods. Then, in keeping with the political propaganda in the myth, the gods construct Esagila, temple tower of Marduk, and Marduk is made chief of all Babylonian gods (8). The text of the myth reads: "They bound him (Kingu) and held him in prison before Ea; they inflicted punishment upon him by cutting open [the arteries of] his blood. With his blood they fashioned mankind . . . After Ea, the wise, had created man [and] had imposed the service of the gods upon him, that work was past understanding."

the Babylonian calendar. Tablet six gives the account of how Kingu, commander-in-chief of Tiamat's forces, is made "scapegoat" and blamed for Tiamat's rebellion. Kingu is executed and the god, Ea, acting on the wishes of his son, Marduk, creates man from Kingu's blood. Man is assigned to serve the gods and a great banquet is held in Marduk's honor.

Tablet seven records Marduk's advancement from chief god of Babylon to headship over all gods in Babylonia.*

What are the differences between Genesis 1 and the Enuma Elish?

While there are similarities between the Enuma Elish and Genesis 1, there are many differences. To begin with, the Babylonian myth is not meant to be essentially an account of creation. It is political propaganda to advance the cause of Babylon in her bid for supremacy in the Mesopotamian world. Genesis presents an account of creation by one God, with no political overtones.

The gross and ridiculous polytheism of the Enuma Elish is obvious. The Babylonian gods are personifications of men who lust, hate and kill with gusto. It is also interesting to note that the Babylonian gods "bleed" and the idea of creating the sky and the earth from seperate halves of one of the dead bodies requires no commentary.

Genesis has no such ridiculous elements. God is God, and there is no implication that He is some sort of glorified man. On the contrary, Genesis I describes how God made man in His own image instead of being made in man's image as is the case with the gods of the Babylonian myth.

Another major difference is that the Babylonian ac-

**See Archaeology and the Old Testament, Merrill F. Unger, Zonder-van Publishing House, 1954, pp. 28-31.

count contains the concept that divine spirit and cosmic matter are co-existent and co-eternal. The Bible, on the other hand, makes it plain that God, an infinite spirit, is creator of all matter.

Although there is a parallel between the seven Babylonian tablets and the seven creative days of Genesis, tablets two and three do not mention any phase of creation. In the Genesis account, God created the firmament on the second day, and on the third day He separated the dry land from the seas and had the earth bring forth grass and trees (Gen. 1:6-13).

But how do Bible scholars account for the similarities between Babylonian myths and Genesis?

There are vast differences between Babylonian myths* and Genesis 1, but many striking similarities are also evident. Most liberal higher critics accept the view that the Hebrews borrowed from the Babylonians and "purified" the account of polytheistic elements, but not all scholars agree.**

For example, although not a holder of the conservative view of inspired Scripture, Jack Finegan recognizes that the differences between the Enuma Elish and Genesis are much more important than any similarities. Finegan believes that certain features of the Biblical narrative are derived from the Babylonian myth or perhaps *"back of both Israelite and Babylonian thought*

---

*In addition to the Enuma Elish (creation myth) other Babylonian myths include the Myth of Adapa, which parallels the fall of man in Genesis 3, and the Gilgamesh Epic, which parallels the flood in Genesis 6-9. For a good description of these myths and their differences and similarities regarding the Genesis accounts, see **Archaeology and the Old Testament,** Merrill F. Unger, Zondervan Publishing House, 1954, chapters 2-5. For another good explanation, see **Genesis and Archaeology** (paperback), Howard F. Vos, Moody Press, 1963, chapters 2-4.

According to Howard Vos (p. 43 of **Genesis and Archaeology), Alexander Heidel, University of Chicago, has made extensive studies that show the "borrowing from the Babylonians" is not the only explanation.

*are some common sources."** (Editor's italics.)

Conservative Bible scholars, such as Merrill F. Unger, believe that Genesis 1 and the Babylonian creation myth *go back to a common source.*** The common elements in the two accounts point to a time when the human race occupied a common home and held a common faith. In other words, the similarities in the two accounts are due to a common heritage and the various races handed on their own version of what happened.

Over the centuries the original pure account got twisted and changed by such peoples as the Babylonians. The Hebrew account, however, is a pure preservation of the original tradition.

Moses wrote the Pentateuch around 1400 B.C. But the event he describes in Genesis 1 through 9—the creation, the fall, and the flood—happened long, long before that. None of these events, in fact, can be dated precisely.

The Babylonian accounts were written no earlier than 2000 B.C. Somewhere, back beyond 2000 B.C. is an original common source of these narratives. The conservative Christian believes that the original common source was God Himself and that He revealed these narratives to Moses in their pure form as the Holy Spirit moved Moses to write the inspired text of Genesis.

Can studying Babylonian myths harm a Christian's faith?

Some Christians might be tempted to claim that there is no value in studying the Babylonian myths, that it could even "undermine" a believer's faith. While there is no spiritual value in the Babylonian myths, they

*See **Light from the Ancient Past,** Jack Finegan, Princeton University Press, p. 65.
See **Archaeology and the Old Testament, Unger, p. 37.

help the Christian gain a better understanding of his Bible. He also gains insight on the criticisms that are directed at Scripture by the person who prefers to disbelieve in the supernatural and the inspiration of God's Word.

A person's view of the validity of the Bible depends on how he wants to view it. Neither the Christian nor the non-Christian can "prove his case." There simply isn't enough evidence. In the final analysis it must be a step of faith. The non-Christian scholar has "faith" in his own human reasoning and keeps Christianity cut down to just another "religion." He also keeps the God of Christianity cut down to size as just "another god."

The Christian, however, takes the leap of faith that Peter talked about in II Peter 1:16: "For we have not depended on made-up legends in making known to you the mighty coming of our Lord Jesus Christ."*

Peter knew Jesus Christ personally. His personal relationship with Jesus Christ convinced him of the validity of Scripture. He was certain that Christianity is based on fact—not fiction.

It is true that there is much in the first chapter of Genesis that we can't understand or explain. As Old Testament scholar Edward J. Young points out, "There is, however, one thing that, by the grace of the Creator, we may do. We may earnestly seek to think the thoughts of God after Him as they are revealed in the mighty first chapter of the Bible. We can cease being rationalists and become believers."**

Non-Christian professors and textbook writers have the privilege and academic freedom to call Bible accounts myths, but *that freedom does not automatically*

*Good News for Modern Man, The New Testament in Today's English Version, American Bible Society, 1966.
**Studies in Genesis One, Edward J. Young, 1964, Presbyterian and Reformed Publishing Co.

prove them correct. The non-Christian professor or higher critical scholar—as well educated as he may be—is making assumptions based on his own information and his own frame of reference. The Christian has no need to apologize for taking a different view—based on *his* information and *his* own frame of reference which centers in faith and trust in a personal God who has revealed Himself in Scripture and in Christ.

Is the Christian's view a biased one? Of course it is. But it is a bias that comes from faith, not doubt, a bias that seeks to know God and acknowledge Him as Lord in humility and obedience.

In the final analysis, it is personal faith and commitment to Jesus Christ that will enable the Christian to stand fast before the non-believer's criticisms of the Bible. No Christian should have his faith depend on how well he can defend the Bible. *His faith is as sound as his relationship to Christ.* This kind of relationship gives the Christian the power and insight of the Holy Spirit. Of this kind of knowledge and power the agnostics and doubters know nothing.

For further reading

Paperbacks

Genesis and Archaeology, Howard F. Vos, Moody Press, 1963. See especially chapters 2-4 on creation, the fall and the flood.

Hardbacks

Archaeology and the Old Testament, Merrill F. Unger, Zondervan Publishing House, 1954. See especially chapters 2-5, which give a detailed analysis of differences and similarities regarding Babylonian myths and the Genesis accounts of creation, the fall of man and the flood.

CHAPTER 8

Is evolution a threat or a theory?

Cardinal Barberini, a friend of Galileo's once explained to him why there should be no conflict between the scientist and the Christian. The Cardinal said, "You teach how the heavens go; we teach how to go to heaven." In other words, science and religion have different aims—they try to answer different questions and do different things for men—so there should be no quarrel between them.

But there is a quarrel—at least some people think so. There are Christians who are sure most scientists are atheists and there are scientists who think most Christians are anti-scientific religious fanatics.

Why is there a so-called "conflict" between science and the Bible?

One of the major reasons for conflict between science and Scripture is a misunderstanding of the purposes of science and the purposes of the Bible. Science is concerned with how things are made and how they work.

The scientist experiments, observes and reports, but the minute he steps over the line to start explaining the "why" and the purpose of the universe and nature, he is out of bounds.

The purpose of the Bible is to reveal God and God's plan for mankind. The Bible is *theological*, that is, it teaches us about God. The Bible tells us why God made the world and mankind.

Science and the Bible, however, are certainly not completely separate from each other. Scripture teaches that God created nature (Gen. 1:1), and that means that God created the very material that the natural scientist studies, tests and observes. God gave man the privilege of studying the world of nature from the beginning (Gen. 1:26-31).

But in today's highly developed technological world, man often substitutes science for God. Some scientists sometimes forget that scientific conclusions are always subject to change. In the world of science, today's "fact" can be tomorrow's "fallacy."*

On the other hand, Christians have been known to hold certain interpretations of the Bible that are in apparent conflict with the findings of science. Christians have also made the mistake of confusing the criticisms of non-believing scientists with the real purpose of science, which is to study God's creation and aid man in the use of the earth as God has commanded. Christianity has nothing to fear from science because the laws of nature and science are of God and it follows that what God has created cannot be of any danger to the Christian's faith in Him.

---

*For example, scientists were once very sure of the existence of a substance called "luminiferous ether" which was supposed to be everywhere and in everything. Scientists also believed that an ingredient called "phlogiston" had to be present in order to produce fire. Both of these views, which many scientists thought to be "unshakable truths," have long since been discarded.

Unfortunately, however, some scientific findings have been interpreted as threats to Christianity. One of the most famous is the theory of organic evolution, which was first put into understandable form for the public by Charles Darwin.

What is Darwin's theory of organic evolution?

Darwin's book, *The Origin of Species by Natural Selection* (published in 1859) "put evolution on the map" as far as the typical man on the street was concerned. Evolutionary theories had been held for hundreds of years, but while men tried to explain the universe by "natural" means, they could not devise a system that really made sense.

Darwin's system, however, did make sense to many people, especially in 1859, a day of extreme rationalism and a time when the Bible was under serious attack by higher critics, who discarded any mention of the supernatural.*

Darwin began by noting that there is variation in all living things. For instance, no two humans are exactly alike. (No, not even identical twins!) Darwin also pointed out that living things are often in competition for food, for living space, for mates. Sometimes a certain variation gives members of a species an advantage over others who don't have that variation. The individuals with the favorable variation (which might make them stronger, healthier, or more capable of fighting or escaping enemies) are likely to win the struggle for existence and they live and reproduce while the others die.

Darwin called this struggle "natural selection," and in popular usage the term led to the phrase "survival of

*For definition and discussion regarding higher critical and rationalistic views of the Bible see chapters 3, 4 and 7.

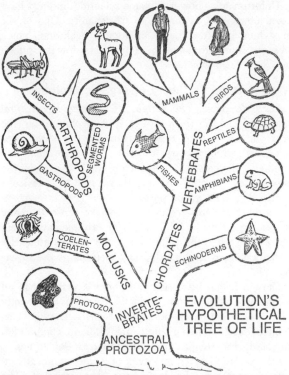

The evolutionist's theory is based on observation of known creatures (see circles on "tree" above) and then "connecting" these
creatures on a hypothetical "tree of life," even though there is
no satisfactory explanation of how this "tree" grew its different
branches. The above is an example of the kind of diagram used
through the first half of the 20th century in textbooks and
encyclopedias.

the fittest." Darwin compared natural selection to
artificial selection, in which a breeder chooses plants or
animals with useful variations and breeds them through
several generations. By "controlled" selection a breeder
tries to develop new varieties that always exhibit certain
favorable variations.

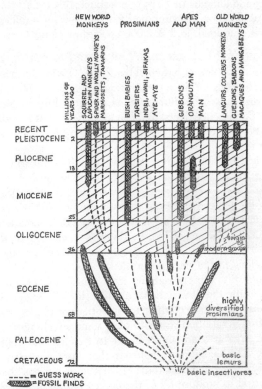

NEW WORLD MONKEYS
PROSIMIANS
APES AND MAN
OLD WORLD MONKEYS

SQUIRREL AND CAPUCHIN MONKEYS
SPIDER AND WOOLLY MONKEYS
MARMOSETS, TAMARINS
BUSH BABIES
TARSIERS
INDRI, AVAHI, SIFAKAS
AYE-AYE
GIBBONS
ORANGUTAN
MAN
LANGURS, COLOBUS MONKEYS
GUENONS, BABOONS
MACAQUES AND MANGABEYS

MILLIONS OF YEARS AGO

RECENT
PLEISTOCENE — 2
PLIOCENE — 13
MIOCENE — 25
OLIGOCENE — 36
EOCENE — 58
PALEOCENE
CRETACEOUS — 72

origin of modern groups

highly diversified prosimians

basic lemurs

basic insectivores

- - - - = GUESS WORK
▨▨▨▨ = FOSSIL FINDS

Above is an example of the newer, more tentative type of "evolutionary tree" but can be found in recent publications (late 1950's and 1960's). Instead of boldly asserting that all life began with some simple forms and then grew on one tree, today's evolutionists prefer to trace the evolution of a certain order such as the primate. Note that there are significant breaks in the various branches, showing that there are tremendous unknown areas where evidence of relationship has not been found.

According to Darwin, natural selection had gone much farther. Darwin believed that from one or a few simple original forms natural selection had produced every species of animal that ever existed. (Counting the

107

plants and animals that are now extinct, this means that natural selection has supposedly accounted for a million species of animals and 250,000 species of plants.)

How is "natural selection" supposed to work?

There is some argument about this. Obviously many characteristics of living things are acquired. That is, they are caused by differences in climate, differences in food, disease, accidents, and the like. Most (but not all) scientists believe that "acquired" characteristics are not inherited.

Scientists also believe that certain characteristics in living things are caused by "genetic mutations." Every living cell contains genes. Genes are tiny units of hereditary information and they determine what individuals in the next generation will be like. But, sometimes a mutation occurs. That is, there is a change in the property (makeup) of a gene. This mutation causes variations in the next generation.

Ironically, most variations are harmful and creatures born with these variations usually die off or do not reproduce. But, according to evolutionary theory, ever so often a variation seems to offer some advantages and these creatures are more likely to survive and reproduce. The evolutionist believes that over a period of many years enough of these "favorable variations" have occurred to produce all of the extinct and living species of plants and animals.

Exactly how does Darwin's theory of organic evolution contradict the Bible?

"Evolution" is a simple word that has become a loaded term. Evolution means "the unfolding" or "orderly development" of something. But Darwin believed in total organic evolution, which has many implications, especially for the person who has faith in the revelation

EVOLUTION BECAME A "RELIGION"

The 19th century was a time of skepticism and rationalism when many men were ready to embrace completely the theory of organic evolution advanced by Lamarck, Darwin and DeVries. Of the three men, Darwin was by far the most influential due to his epic work, **The Origin of Species.** Darwin's book popularized the concept of evolution and gave men another explanation for the origin of life, which led to evolutionism, a type of religious humanism that substitutes natural selection for God.

of God's Word, the Bible.

A one time divinity student, Darwin was no atheist by any means. In the final paragraph of his book, *The Origin of Species,* he speaks of ". . . life, with its several powers, having been originally breathed by the Creator into a few forms or into one. . . "*

Darwin, however, found it hard to conceive of "fixity of species"—that is, a Creator going through innumerable acts of creation in order to produce the hundreds of

---

*The Origin of Species, Charles Darwin, Mentor Paperback Edition, 1958, p. 450.

thousands of species of various plants and animals that have ever existed. But in reacting to the "fixity of species" interpretation of the Bible that was prevalent in his day, Darwin devised a theory that—followed to its ultimate logical conclusion—leaves no room for, and has no need of, a Creator. In other words, Darwin's theory left so much to chance and "natural selection" that it was easy for the anti-supernaturalists of his day to use the theory of organic evolution to rule God out of the picture completely.

George Bernard Shaw, one of the outstanding playwrights of all time, once mentioned that Darwin's theory became public at a time when the world was "fed up" with the notion that everything had happened through the "arbitrary personal act of an arbitrary personal God, of dangerous, jealous and cruel personal character . . ." and that is why many people literally jumped at Darwin's theory and took it far beyond the realm of science and literally made it a religion.[*]

The controversy between Christianity and the theory of organic evolution is a good example of how men can react against theological dogma which is not necessarily what the Scriptures actually teach. Even though the evidence for evolution was not convincing at that time (and it is still not convincing) men accepted it as a dogma to be believed by faith because here at last was one plausible explanation for the world and living things that could be an alternative to the idea of divine intervention.

Do variations and changes in plants and animals prove Darwin's theory of organic evolution?

In the past, people thought that the Bible taught "fixity of species," that is, that God created every single

[*]See **Darwin, Evolution and Creation,** edited by Paul Zimmerman, Concordia Publishing House, 1959, pp. 21, 22.

species and that all of these species had never changed. This was originally the belief of Linnaeus, the eighteenth century "father of taxonomy," who developed a system of classifying plants and animals. Linnaeus later changed his ideas on "fixity of species", but as is often the case, his error continued to be taught long after he had corrected his views. There are many evolutionists today who think that if a Christian opposes the theory of organic evolution it is because he supports the idea of fixity of species.

But what does the Bible say? The Bible does not use the word "species" but instead says that God created living things "after their kind." (See Genesis 1:21.)

For example, the Bible mentions "the owl ... after his kind" (Leviticus 11:16). But the owl is not just a species. The owl is an entire "order" (strigiformes), so the "kind" obviously can include a number of species. The point is that God could have created "one kind" of owl that later developed into several different species.

Going back to Genesis for a moment, some of the "kinds" mentioned in chapter one are grass, fruit trees, fowl, fish, cattle, and of course, "mankind." There are, of course, many species of most of these and certainly there are many "varieties" of men. So, the fact of change and variation in living things is certainly no proof that Darwin's theory is right and the Bible is wrong. There is no justification for equating the "kinds" of Genesis with biological species.

What about the "record of the rocks"? Do fossils prove evolution?

Fossils are remains or traces of things that lived ages ago. Fossils are found in rock strata that lie one upon the other much like the layers of a cake. How long ago did these forms live?

Since the first part of the twentieth century, scientists

have been using radioactive methods of dating the age of the rocks and the fossils. Some of these methods include Uranium-Lead, Potassium-Argon and Carbon-14. All radioactive dating methods are based upon the principle that there are certain elements within fossils or rocks that are decaying at a certain rate of speed. Through the use of highly technical equipment and complicated formulas, the scientist can measure the amount of a decaying element in a rock or a fossil such as a skull, and then, by computing the known rate of decay of that particular element, he can arrive at the fossil's approximate age.

For example, about 0.001 percent of every sample of natural Potassium is an element called Potassium-40. Scientists calculate that it takes 1.25 billion years for half of this Potassium to decay into Calcium-40 and Argon-40. So, to determine the age of the sample, the scientists measure how much Potassium-40 has changed into Argon-40.

From such studies, scientists believe that many fossils have been discovered in rocks that are millions of years old and the age of the earth itself is estimated at billions of years.*

Potassium-Argon dating is used to estimate great periods of time going back millions of years. Carbon-14 is used to date fossils and the fossils of more recent vintage—60,000 years old or less.

Developed by W. F. Libby, an American physicist, the Carbon-14 method is based on the principle that cosmic rays are entering the earth's upper atmosphere and producing Carbon-14 atoms that are eventually absorbed by the waters of the earth and used by growing plants. Animals that feed upon these plants

*For a good discussion of the strengths and weaknesses in radioactive dating methods see Chapter 5, "The Age of the Earth," by Paul Zimmerman, Darwin, Evolution and Creation, Concordia Publishing House, 1959, pp. 142-166.

absorb some Carbon-14. In fact, Carbon-14 is one of the radioactive materials in your own body.

Living things such as plants, trees and animals absorb fresh Carbon-14 constantly until they die. But at death the process of absorption stops and Carbon-14 in the organism disintegrates at a certain rate. According to Dr. Libby, the "half life" of Carbon-14 is 5,568 years, which means that in a fossil that has been preserved for that amount of time half of the Carbon-14 will have disintegrated. Scientists can measure the amount of radioactivity due to Carbon-14 in a fossil and from this they can determine how old a fossil is. For example, if they find that the Carbon-14 in the fossil is one-fourth of its normal level the fossil is "two half lives" old—that is 11,200 years.

Carbon-14 has been tested successfully on samples of known age—for example, on Redwood trees and on wood used in the tombs of the Pharaohs of Egypt. On the other hand, there have been tests of Carbon-14 that have turned out to be negative and the computed dates have been inaccurate. Scientists continue to work with Carbon-14 as well as other radioactive dating methods with a fair amount of assurance that the methods are reliable but only within certain limits.*

While dating methods have not proven to be absolutely precise, the general feeling in the scientific world is that they are reliable, and many Christians in scientific occupations accept the dates as "accurate." The question is, does a great age of the earth (whether it be 100,000, 1,000,000 or 5,000,000,000 years old) prove the theory of organic evolution? The evolutionist claims that it does because he points to a fossil record that suggests change in development in living things over great periods of time. The evolutionist believes this is proof that life began with a single cell, progressed to simple forms of life, then during vast ages of time

*See Darwin, Evolution and Creation, pp. 156-161.

evolved into present forms of life on earth today.

There are, however, missing chapters in the evolutionist's "record of the rocks." According to the theory of organic evolution, science should be able to discover life forms dating back to the earliest geologic periods that are supposed to have supported life (the Archeozoic and Proterozoic eras dated one billion to two billion years ago). Instead, however, the fossil record shows almost no life forms until the "Cambrian period" of 500 million years ago. The so-called "Cambrian explosion" of at least nine or ten different life forms puzzles evolutionists. Even though they have found evidence of a few life forms before the Cambrian period (algae and certain kinds of worms) they have not found the required transitional "missing links" between the Cambrian period and earlier pre-Cambrian times.

The evolutionist explains the lack of these transitional fossils by claiming that before the time of the Cambrian period the geological column (that is, the series of strata or layers of rock) shows much "disconformity." The term, "disconformity," means that rock layers were laid down, eroded and destroyed and then covered by more new layers. This disruption, claim evolutionists, probably destroyed any transitional fossils that did exist.

The word "probably" is the key here. The evolutionist has no proof that there were such fossils and that they were destroyed. He is going on his theory and making assumptions and deductions accordingly.

It is interesting to note that Darwin himself did not think fossils gave much support for his theory of organic evolution by natural selection. The missing links in the fossil record were of particular concern to Darwin and he even wrote an entire chapter in *The Origin of Species* entitled, "On the Imperfection of the Geological Record."

In addition to the puzzle of the Cambrian explosion,

THE CAMBRIAN EXPLOSION
PUZZLES EVOLUTIONISTS

ERA	PERIOD	EPOCH	SUCCESSION OF LIFE
CENOZOIC "Recent life"	QUATERNARY 1 million years	Recent Pleistocene	
CENOZOIC "Recent life"	TERTIARY 60 million years	Pliocene Miocene Oligocene Eocene Paleocene	
MESOZOIC "Middle life"	CRETACEOUS 70 million years	Late Early	
MESOZOIC "Middle life"	JARUSSIC 25 million years	Late Middle Early	
MESOZOIC "Middle life"	TRIASSIC 30 million years	Late Middle Early	
PALEOZOIC "Ancient life"	PERMIAN 25 million years	Late Middle Early	
PALEOZOIC "Ancient life"	PENNSYLVANIAN 25 million years (CARBONIFEROUS)	No formal subdivisions	
PALEOZOIC "Ancient life"	MISSISSIPPIAN 30 million years	No formal subdivisions	
PALEOZOIC "Ancient life"	DEVONIAN 55 million years	Late Middle Early	
PALEOZOIC "Ancient life"	SILURIAN 40 million years	Late Middle Early	Cambrian Explosion of Many Life Forms
PALEOZOIC "Ancient life"	ORDOVICIAN 80 million years	Late Middle Early	Cambrian Explosion of Many Life Forms
PALEOZOIC "Ancient life"	CAMBRIAN 80 million years	Late Middle Early	Cambrian Explosion of Many Life Forms
PRE-CAMBRIAN ERAS More than 2 billion 100 million years			Pre-Cambrian Period Shows Few Forms of Life
PROTEROZOIC ERA			Pre-Cambrian Period Shows Few Forms of Life
ARCHEOZOIC ERA			

APPROXIMATE AGE OF THE EARTH MORE THAN 2 BILLION 600 MILLION YEARS

GEOLOGICAL TIME SCALE

Above is a typical geological time scale showing the various geological eras and periods (column at left) and the types of life
forms that appeared during these various time spans. Until the
dawn of the Cambrian period (80 million years ago) fossil discoveries show few life forms, but suddenly at least nine or ten
different life forms appear in fully developed form. This puzzles
evolutionists because, according to their theory, life forms should
have been developing in great abundance in the pre-Cambrian
times as well.

the evolutionist also faces the lack of transitional fossil
forms from the time of the Cambrian period until the
present day. Very few forms of any kind have been
found in the fossil record that can be called transitional
—that is, halfway between one kind of living thing and

another. An example that evolutionists often refer to as a transitional form is the Archaeopteryx (ark-a-op-ter-ix). Some scientists claim this creature was part reptile and part bird but others disagree and say that it in no way bridges the gap between the two groups.

Evolutionists try to explain the lack of transitional fossil forms by saying that preservation of fossils is very rare and requires certain conditions that are seldom present over much of the earth. The creationists reply that although a great deal of fossil evidence has been dug up, the missing links are still missing. Although the evolutionist asserts that the fossil record supports his case, he still lacks a great deal of evidence to conclusively prove the theory of organic evolution from "amoeba to man."

"Ontogeny Recapitulates Phylogeny" or —HOW'S THAT AGAIN?

This is sometimes called the embryological argument for Darwin's theory. It simply states that the embryo of a living creature repeats the whole process of evolution up to that stage. For example, take mammals, creatures with warm blood, solid bones, lungs that breathe air, and they nourish their young with milk. According to Darwin's theory, the ancestor of all mammals was a little sea-dwelling creature that had a gristly rod instead of a backbone. What's the proof? Very simple. As we follow the development of a mammal embryo, it first has a gristly rod which becomes cartilage and finally bone. At the same time, the embryo develops gills like a fish, loses them, then builds up two lungs. The embryo's heart first resembles that of a fish, then later becomes the four-chambered pump common to adult animals.

Is this "proof" of evolution? Darwin and another scientist, Ernest Haeckel, believed that it was, but a lot of people have disagreed with them since then. For one thing, it was found that some of Haeckel's comparative diagrams were not entirely honest. For another thing— far more important—it is now recognized that the resemblances of the human embryo to a fish (for example) are very superficial. The human embryo never really has "gills." These are actually "pharyngeal pouches" that will develop into important structures such as the ear chamber, tonsils, parathyroid glands and thymus.

Instead of saying that embryos show stages of adult forms that supposedly preceded them in evolution, most biologists now simply say that the embryos of many creatures show similarities. Certainly these similarities do not "prove" evolution. The Christian has every right to maintain that the Creator used a perfect "master plan" for the development of mammals in embryo form.

Does comparative anatomy prove Darwin's theory?

Evolutionists point out that just as embryos are similar there are also similarities between fully grown creatures. Take a human arm, a whale's flipper, the front leg of an alligator, the wing of a bat. They all show the same basic arrangement of bone and muscles, blood vessels and nerves. Those who place their faith in Darwin's theory say that this shows that these creatures are related—that they descend from a common ancestor. The Christian creationist can just as easily suggest that all these features had the same Creator who (just as in the development of various embryos) used a similar pattern and master plan.

What about those extra parts?

Evolutionists used to point with confidence to certain organs that now seem to have no function. These organs have been called vestigial organs and evolutionists suggest that the creature possessing them is descended from some other creature who found them useful. In man, for example, lists of vestigial organs have included the pituitary gland, tonsils and the appendix. These were once thought to have no useful function in the human body. Unfortunately for the evolutionist's argument, the list of vestigial organs has shrunk radically since Darwin's time. Today the pituitary gland is considered one of the most important in the human body. Doctors no longer remove tonsils at an early age because they now believe that tonsils help fight infection.

In view of modern findings, vestigial organs (which perhaps should now be called "organs of unknown function") are hardly a "proof" of Darwin's theory of organic evolution.

Is genetics the "mechanism" of organic evolution?

Genetics is the science of studying the traits, physical characteristics and properties that can be passed along from parent to offspring. Because Darwin developed his theories before the discovery of the science of genetics, he believed that evolution depended on the natural selection of the characteristics best suited to survive. But Hugo DeVries, a Dutch botanist, developed the theory that changes in living things come about due to mutations—changes within the genes.

Today genetics is considered by many evolutionists to be the "mechanism" of evolution—that is, the way evolutionary changes occur through natural selection. Geneticists carry on many experiments, with x-ray for example, and produce actual changes in the genes of certain organisms. But there is no evidence to date that these gene changes (mutations) ever result in a new form of life. No observed genetic change is adequate to prove the concept that fishes turned to frogs and reptiles

DOES CHANGE WITHIN SPECIES PROVE EVOLUTION?

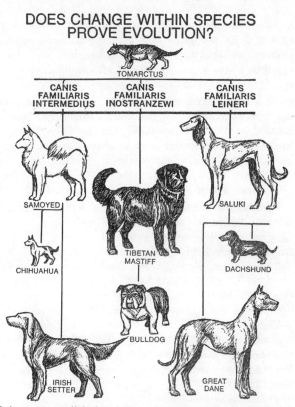

TOMARCTUS

CANIS FAMILIARIS INTERMEDIUS   CANIS FAMILIARIS INOSTRANZEWI   CANIS FAMILIARIS LEINERI

SAMOYED

CHIHUAHUA

TIBETAN MASTIFF

SALUKI

DACHSHUND

BULLDOG

IRISH SETTER

GREAT DANE

Today many evolutionists believe that the "mechanism" of evolution is genetic mutation combined with natural selection. But no genetic mutation to date has ever resulted in a completely new kind of living organism. The above diagram shows how various species of the dog have descended from a prototype called "Tomarctus." Only a few dogs from each species are shown on this diagram, which is adapted from a much more extensive chart appearing in **Evolution**, Life Nature Library, Time, Inc., pp. 86, 87. Despite the vast differences in various sub-species of dogs, from the tiny Chihuahua to the giant Great Dane, they are still all dogs. Genetic changes (whether induced by "natural selection" or by artificial breeding methods used by man) provide absolutely no proof for the theory of organic macro-evolution.

to birds as evolutionists claim happened in the distant past. That there has been change within species (for example, the dog or the horse) is obvious. But such change does not prove the assumption made by the believer in organic evolution—that great leaps and changes were accomplished, which resulted in completely new forms of life.

In acknowledging that mutations and changes have occurred in living things, creationists (those who believe in God as Creator) recognize that "micro-evolution"— evolution within species and in some cases up to the genera* of a family has occurred. But this does not mean that the creationist accepts "macro-evolution," which means large change above the genera level.

Genetic evidence and experiments indicate that organisms reproduce "after their kind" and this is precisely what the Bible says: "And God said, let the earth bring forth the living creature after his kind . . ." (Gen. 1:24). The Scriptures translate the Hebrew word *"min"* as "kind." Exactly what "kind" means is a subject of discussion by Bible scholars. There is, however, no justification for equating the "kinds" of Genesis with biological species.

Geneticist John W. Klotz observes, "There is still no reason for departing from the Scriptural provision for limited change within the 'kinds' created at the beginning."**

Theistic evolution—can you have your cake and eat it, too?

Despite the lack of final proof for macro-evolution, there are people (many of whom are in church circles)

---

*A species is a group of similar organisms. A genus is a group of closely related species. A family is a group of closely related genera. An order is a group of related families. A class is a group of related orders. A phylum is a group of related orders—the largest grouping in the animal or plant kingdoms.
**See "Theistic Evolution: Some Theological Implications," John W. Klotz, Journal of the American Scientific Affiliation, Sept. 1963, pp. 93, 84.

who find it difficult to reconcile the language of Genesis 1 with modern science. These people seek to stand on a middle ground called "theistic evolution." There are several definitions of theistic evolution but the most widely held view is that God created the first cell and used organic evolution to produce all the species that have developed since.*

The theistic evolutionist who wishes to hold the position that God created the first cell and everything else evolved thereafter through natural selection and genetic mutation usually looks on Genesis 1 as "poetry" or "myth." As geneticist John Klotz points out, "Theistic evolutionists recognize that a literal interpretation of Genesis cannot be accommodated . . ."**

The point is this: If you try to explain Genesis 1 by saying "God worked through evolution" you leave yourself wide open to the liberal and neo-orthodox higher critical view of the Bible which denies its inspiration and infallibility. In addition you set yourself at odds with the firmly stated opinions of Christ himself who obviously took Genesis just as seriously as any other part of Scripture. For example, Christ spoke of man's special creation as a historical fact when He was discussing marriage: "Have ye not read, that he which made them at the beginning made them male and female?" (Matt. 19:4).

Acceptance of theistic macro-evolution also brings up serious questions about the reality of sin and the need

---

*Other interpretations of theistic evolution include: (1) God created the first cell and organic evolution took over the process of developing life up to the level of man, where God intervened to create man by breathing the breath of life into some highly developed animal. (2) God created the first life form or forms and then also intervened at various stages to create other forms that then evolved within their own family or order. This second view is very close to the creationist position, which holds that God created living things "after their kind."

**See "Theistic Evolution: Some Theological Implications," *Journal of the ASA*, Sept. 1963, pp. 83, 84.

for redemption from sin. The Bible presents Jesus Christ in His primary role as personal Saviour from sin and as Lord of all who believe. See for example, John 3:16; Romans 3:22; I Cor. 15:3, 4; I Peter 3:18. But if man is only an animal evolving from some other kind of animal, then sin tends to be merely lack of adequate development. The gospel of redemption from sin tends to have no meaning.

No Christian should feel he has to dwell in the "halfway house" of theistic evolution. Darwin's theory of organic evolution is still only a theory. The problem is that many popular periodicals (*Life* magazine is a prime example), encyclopedias and textbooks on biology imply or even openly assert that, because of evidence for micro-evolution, macro-evolution "must be the way all life happened to develop." In other words, the writers of these articles and textbooks are saying that they do not want to believe in God's divine creative act and that they have to find a natural explanation for life itself.

As was pointed out earlier in this chapter, the basic question is not the Bible versus science. The basic question is *naturalism* versus *supernaturalism, rationalism* versus *faith in the living God.*

Organic evolution is no threat to the Christian faith. In fact, the organic evolutionist exercises strong faith of his own to believe that his viewpoint is the explanation for how living things came into existence. The evolutionist's hypothetical "tree of life" contains a great deal of "hypothetical wood."

The Christian need make no apology for standing on what he feels is far firmer ground. The Christian points to God's revelation through the Bible and affirms that in the beginning God (not some cosmic accident) created the heaven and the earth. There is much the Christian does not know, and much that he will never know this side of eternity. But the Christian does know that he can turn to Scripture with the assurance that comes through faith in Christ and believe that God created living things "after their kind," and He created man in His own image, with a living soul (Gen. 1:24, 26; 2:7).

For further reading
Paperbacks

Darwin, Evolution, and Creation, edited by Paul A. Zimmerman, Concordia Publishing House, 1959. A symposium by several writers who present the issues between conservative biblical Christianity and the theory of organic evolution in readable objective style. Includes chapters on the history of Darwinism, creation, the case for and against evolution, the age of the earth, and the influence of Darwinism on society today.

Evolution, Fact or Theory? Cora A. Reno, Moody Press, 1953. Dr. Reno examines several of the basic arguments for evolution and then presents the counter-arguments from the biblical point of view. The author is familiar with the typical teaching of evolution in public schools, which often implies that evolution is a fact, not a theory.

Science Speaks, Peter W. Stoner, Moody Press, 1958. See especially chapter 1 concerning scientific accuracy and scientific problems. Dr. Stoner's manuscript was carefully reviewed by a committee from the American Scientific Affiliation, a group of over 400 Christian men in all fields of science.

Faith and the Physical World, David L. Dye, William B. Eerdmans Publishing Company, 1966. A holder of a Ph.D. in physics, Dr. Dye examines many facets of the Christian's relationship to the world he lives in. For information on evolution, see chapter 5, pp. 136-150.

The Origin of Species, Charles Darwin, Mentor Paperback Edition, New American Library, 1958. A republished version of Darwin's history-making work, with a special introduction by Sir Julian Huxley, twentieth century humanist and champion of neo-Darwinism.

The Case For Creation, Wayne Frair, P. William Davis, Moody Press, 1967. See especially chapters 1-4, which deal with the basic theory of organic evolution.

Darwin: Before and After, Robert E. D. Clark, Moody

Press, paperback edition, 1967. Gives good background on Darwin and provides a fascinating summary of Darwin's thinking as he developed his theory of organic evolution through natural selection.

Hardbacks

The Bible, Science and Creation, S. Maxwell Coder, George F. Howe, Moody Press, 1965. See especially chapters 4-7 which deal with the Bible and science, origins and the evidence for special creation by God.

Genes, Genesis and Evolution, John W. Klotz, Concordia Publishing House, 1955. A thorough study in the theory of organic evolution by a trained geneticist, who believes that the evidence points to micro-evolution within species but clearly refutes the assumption of the organic evolutionist that macro-evolution (large jumps between major groups and orders) has occurred.

Creation Revealed, F. A. Filby, Fleming H. Revell Company, 1964. A convinced Christian who is an instructor in inorganic chemistry in a college in England, Dr. Filby probes the assumption of organic evolution with searching questions. See for example pp. 79-83, 108-109.

Implications of Evolution, G. A. Kerkut, Pergamon Press, 1960. Not written from the Christian viewpoint, this book still challenges the theory of organic evolution as an attempt to explain all living forms as coming from a unique source. The introduction and chapter 1 "Basic Assumptions" are especially helpful.

Why We Believe In Creation Not Evolution, Fred John Meldau, Christian Victory Publishing Company, 1959. Contains many interesting illustrations from the world of nature which challenge the basic assumptions in the theory of organic evolution.

Evolution and Christian Thought Today, edited by Russell L. Mixter, William B. Eerdmans Publishing Company, 1959. A symposium by twelve scientists covering such areas as biology, origin of the universe, genetics, prehistoric man, and a closing chapter on theology and evolution by Carl F. H. Henry, long time editor of *Christianity Today*.

CHAPTER 9
How did man get here and why?

Until fairly recent times, most people thought of man as essentially different from the animals. From the time of Plato until well into the nineteenth century, it was generally believed that only man is rational. This would agree exactly with the first chapter of Genesis which describes the creation of man. Man is presented as more than an animal. He is a person, "a living soul," created "in the image of God." All this is completely contradicted by Darwin's theory.

Darwin believed that man and the ape came from a common ancestor. He believed that man and the ape differ only in degree, not in kind. Man's rationality is the product of blind irrational evolution. Even man's sense of right and wrong, says Darwin, came into existence this way. Darwin writes ". . . the first foundation or origin of the moral sense lies in the social instincts ... these instincts no doubt were primarily gained, as in the case of the lower animals, through natural selection."* Darwin says, "no doubt," but is the

---

*The Descent of Man, Charles Darwin, p. 914, Modern Library edition published in one volume with Darwin's The Origin of Species.

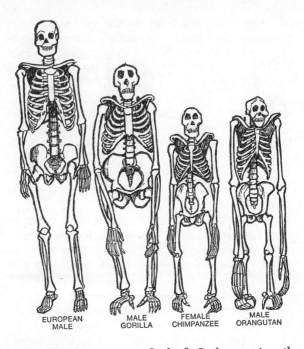

EUROPEAN
MALE

MALE
GORILLA

FEMALE
CHIMPANZEE

MALE
ORANGUTAN

case really that open and shut? Let's examine the evidence carefully.

Does man's similarity to apes prove evolution?

Similarity between man and ape is still a major piece of evidence offered as evidence for evolution. The evolutionist suggests that the skeletons of men, gorillas, chimpanzees, orangutans and gibbons all show similar structural characteristics and that therefore they must be related to a "common ancestor."

The creationist replies that the similarities could just as easily point to a Common Designer who used certain basic structures that are best for certain creatures.

The creationist also points to the vast mental gulf between men and apes. Even Julian Huxley, twentieth century champion of evolution, admits that the supposed great leap over the gap between the ape and man occurred only once and could never take place again.*

Creationists also note that although there are similarities between apes and men, there are many differences. Only man walks upright on two legs. Apes, contrary to popular belief, seldom walk on their hind legs and usually move about on all fours. There are many other differences in bone structures, such as the "thumbs" on an ape's feet as well as his hands.

But above all, Klotz, like many other scientists, observes that only man is teachable. You can train an animal such as an ape, but you cannot teach him to exercise independent judgment as human beings can.**

What about the "cave-men" and "man-apes"?

Many interesting fossils have been uncovered in recent years. Some are of extinct species (such as mammoths and dinosaurs). Some seem to be of species that resemble modern man and/or modern apes. The best known of these have been given such names as: Java ape-man (Pithecanthropus erectus), Peking man (Sinanthropus), Swanscombe man, Neanderthal man, Cro-Magnon man. The most recent and best publicized finds are the "man-ape" group (Australopithecus).

---

*See Evolution: The Modern Synthesis, Julian Huxley, Harper and Row, 1942. Huxley believes that if man wipes himself out (by atomic war for example) it is improbable that the step to conceptual thought would be taken by his nearest kin, meaning the apes.
**See Darwin, Creation and Evolution, edited by Paul Zimmerman, Concordia, 1959, p. 128.

25 MILLION YEARS AGO	20	15	10

PLIOPITHECUS

PROCONSUL

DRYOPITHECUS

OREOPITHECUS

RAMAPITHECUS

PLIOPITHECUS PROCONSUL   DRYOPITHECUS OREOPITHECUS RAMAPITHECUS

The above is adapted from the time line chart, "The Road to Homo Sapiens" on pp. 41-45 of **Early Man** by F. Clark Howell (Life Nature Library, Time, Inc., 1965). Evolutionist Howell's chart is a good example of approaching the fossil evidence with pre-conceived ideas that evolution "must be" the way man originated. It is then a simple matter to line up the reconstructed fossils and make a case for your theory. Much of this chart, however, is

Some of these creatures are discussed in the book *Early Man* by F. Clark Howell, professor of anthropology at the University of Chicago. For example, pages 41-45 include a full color fold out chart entitled, "The Road to Homo Sapiens." The chart shows artists' reconstructions of ancient extinct creatures that are arranged in order of complexity from "proto-ape" forms up to modern man.

"For purposes of comparison" the artist shows all of the various forms standing, although Howell admits that many of them were quadrupedal. The overall effect of such a chart is to heavily imply that man evolved from apelike ancestors, although there is no definite proof that this is so.

Many "artists' reconstructions" of fossil discoveries use similar techniques.

Are "reconstructions" of fossils really accurate?

Anthropologist E. A. Hooten pointed out that from a Neanderthal skull an artist could fashion the features of a chimpanzee or that of a philosopher.* Hooten was

*See **Up from the Ape**, E. A. Hooten, Macmillan, 1931, p. 332.

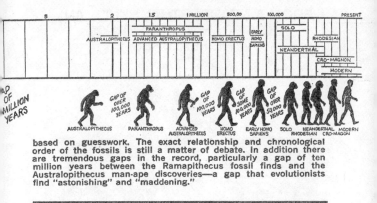

PARANTHROPUS

AUSTRALOPITHECUS   ADVANCED AUSTRALOPITHECUS   HOMO ERECTUS   EARLY HOMO SAPIENS   SOLO

NEANDERTHAL   RHODESIAN

CRO-MAGNON

MODERN

AD OF MILLION YEARS

AUSTRALOPITHECUS   GAP OF OVER 100,000 YEARS   PARANTHROPUS   ADVANCED AUSTRALOPITHECUS   GAP OF 100,000 YEARS   HOMO ERECTUS   GAP OF SOME 100,000 YEARS   EARLY HOMO SAPIENS   GAP OF OVER 50,000 YEARS   SOLO   NEANDERTHAL RHODESIAN   MODERN CRO-MAGON

based on guesswork. The exact relationship and chronological order of the fossils is still a matter of debate. In addition there are tremendous gaps in the record, particularly a gap of ten million years between the Ramapithecus fossil finds and the Australopithecus man-ape discoveries—a gap that evolutionists find "astonishing" and "maddening."

perhaps remembering that when the first Neanderthal skeleton was found, it was reconstructed to suit what its reconstructor, Professor Marcellin Boule, thought that ancient man should look like. As a result, he depicted Neanderthal as stooped over and with an apelike face.

Along with questionable reconstruction, there have also been cases of outright fraud and forgery connected with fossils. Perhaps the best known case came to light in 1953. The story began in 1912 when Charles Dawson announced his discovery of "ape-man" fossils near the town of Piltdown in England. The reconstruction of "Piltdown man" started a raging controversy. The skull appeared to be human; the lower jaw appeared apelike.

Finally, a team of British scientists, Kenneth P. Oakley, J. S. Weiner, and W. E. Le Gros Clark, used modern techniques to test Dawson's fossil finds. Their conclusions were shocking. "Piltdown man" was a careful and cunning forgery. The skull was actually that of a modern man, the jaw was that of a modern ape. The teeth had been filed and stained to make them look different. "Piltdown man" was a fake and scientists had been fooled for forty years.

129

FROM A NEANDERTHAL SKULL, AN ARTIST CAN RECONSTRUCT THE FEATURES

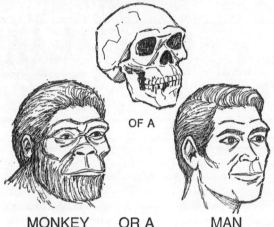

OF A

MONKEY   OR A   MAN

"PUT NOT YOUR FAITH IN RECONSTRUCTIONS"

Above is an example of how a Neanderthal skull can be "reconstructed" in an artist's drawing at a certain angle to look like a monkey or a man. Well-known anthropologist E. A. Hooten has said that from a Neanderthal skull an artist can fashion the features of a chimpanzee or a philosopher and that it is wise to " . . . put not your faith in reconstructions."

All this shows how unreliable and subjective this business can be. Obviously, to take a handful of ancient dried bones and come up with a detailed "artist's reconstruction" requires an enormous amount of guesswork.

"Put not your faith in reconstructions," said Professor Hooten. That's still not bad advice.

Still, "manlike" fossils have been found. These ancient creatures did exist. From South Africa in recent years have come reports of the discoveries of Drs. Louis and

Mary Leakey, who found the fossils of creatures that they believe lived a million or more years ago.* In structure, these creatures seem similar to man. Were they men? Or were they apes? Are they descended from Adam? Are they ancestors of modern man? They seem to have been toolmakers. Do animals ever make tools?

Recent studies have shed light on the ability of animals to make tools. It has been found, for example, that the chimpanzee is both a tool user and a tool-maker. He uses sticks and rocks to dig with and to crack nuts. He finds thin twigs and pokes them into termites' nests. Then he pulls out the twig carefully and eats the insects that cling to it. The chimpanzee even makes "tools" for this purpose, by stripping away the leaves of a twig or vine. He even carries his tools around with him. All this has been noted by Jean Goodall, a chimpanzee expert working in East Africa. She has come to think that chimpanzees learn by watching each other.**

What is the Christian to think of Darwin's theory as applied to man?

The chemist, Anthony Standen, writing in *Science Is a Sacred Cow*, quotes paleontologist R. S. Lull of Yale as follows: "Since Darwin's day evolution has been more and more generally accepted, until now in the minds of informed thinking men there is no doubt that it is the only logical way whereby the creation can be interpreted and understood. We are not so sure, however, as to the modus operandi, but we may rest assured that the process has been in accordance with great natural laws, some of which are as yet unknown, perhaps unknowable."*** Standen wonders how the bi-

*For details on the Leakey discoveries of Australopithecus, see Early Man, F. Clark Howell, Life Nature Library, Time Inc. 1965, pp. 47-75.
**For a fascinating report on Miss Goodall's work, see National Geographic, August 1963.
***Science Is a Sacred Cow, Anthony Standen, Dutton paperback edition, p. 106.

ologist can "rest assured" if these "great natural laws" are "unknown" and "unknowable"? If unknown, how can he be sure they are there? If unknowable, how can he be sure they are "logical"?

Standen also observes that the term "missing link" is misleading because not only one link, but entire chunks of the evolutionary chain are missing. With every new discovery of an ancient "manlike" fossil, the genealogical tree gets more complicated. To date the Darwin theory is unproven. There are some scientists (not necessarily Christians) who feel that to explain living things by evolution is ". . . not satisfactorily supported by present day evidence."[*]

F. A. Filby, senior lecturer in organic chemistry at South-East Essex Technical College in England, points out that with all the controversy about what the fossils mean, Christians ". . . can afford to wait for something a little more definite." Filby, a convinced creationist and Christian, feels there is no real conflict between the essential teaching of the Bible and the known facts of paleontology and anthropology. We are looking at a great jigsaw puzzle, but somehow all the pieces fit together. "Maybe Bible students and scientists, having started from different edges, cannot yet quite see how their pieces will join up to make a complete picture . . . but the conclusion I have come to is that they do."[**]

David F. Siemens, Jr., instructor at Los Angeles Pierce College, comments:

"What makes a creature human cannot be determined from his bones nor even from his tools. It is conceivable that manlike, tool-using non-human species once existed. Indeed, nothing in Scripture rules out the

[*]See **Implications of Evolution**, G. A. Kerkut, Pergamon Press, 1960, p. vii.
[**]**Creation Revealed**, F. A. Filby, Revell, p. 151.

existence of such a species either before or at the same time as the first men. Adam was the first man not because he walked erect nor because he tilled the ground nor even because he could speak, although these involve fundamental characteristics of man, but because he alone received from His Creator the breath of life. This unique gift with its intended God-consciousness was passed on to all his descendants, but never shows up on their bones."

What does "created in God's image" mean?

"Created in God's image" certainly means a wide gulf between man and animals. Man differs from the animals in kind, not merely degree. Man is a unique product of the creative work of God.

According to Scripture, man comes as a climax to God's creative work. (See Gen. 1:26—2:7.) God creates man "in His own image" and breathes into him the breath of life so that man becomes a living soul.

"Created in God's image," means that man was made for a unique relationship with God. The meaning of this kind of relationship is difficult to grasp entirely, but consider for a moment just what man is. Man was created with self-consciousness, feelings, emotions, self determination—a will. Man was given highly developed senses, the ability to think and (most important) a God-consciousness.

"In God's image" also means that man has a spirit of life, a soul, a personality, a mind—all attributes that reflect the infinite qualities of God. Man is a free rational being. Through his own choice man is capable of possessing something of God's knowledge, righteousness and holiness. It is because man is who he is that he is "redeemable from sin"—that is, he can be "saved" in the Biblical sense of the word. This is what Paul meant when he wrote to the Colossian Christians and said,

133

"You are living a brand new kind of life that is ever learning more and more of what is right, and trying to be more and more like Christ Who created this new life within you" (Col. 3:10, *Living Letters*).

The Bible tells us man's body was fashioned from the "dust of the ground" and that man's spirit came from the very "breath of God" (Gen. 2:7). Exactly what "dust" means is a matter of opinion among Bible scholars, but there is no real ground for saying (as some critics suggest) that it means God made a mud pie shaped like a man and then wired it for sight and sound. As any chemistry student knows, a man is made up of certain elements, such as calcium, carbon, oxygen, iron, phosphorus, nitrogen and zinc that would sell for around $2.00. One chemist, who is also an apt Bible scholar, speculates that "dust" might mean that man's body is composed of very fine particles and that this is as close as the Hebrews came to atomic theory.*

At any rate, God communicated His own life to the inert mass of substance He had molded into form. His divine breath permeated the material and transformed it into a living thing. This unique combination of dust and deity produced a marvelous creation made in God's own image.**

"Created in God's image" also means man is here for a purpose—to be the steward (caretaker) of all of God's creation. God commissioned man to rule over nature in Gen. 1:28-31.

What qualities were needed to fulfill this task of having dominion over all the earth? Certainly the mind, personality, and self determination qualities in man equip him for this job, which is far beyond the reach of any animal. As Mortimer Adler has pointed out, man

*See **Creation Revealed**, F. A. Filby, Revell, 1964, pp. 118, 119.
See **Wycliffe Bible Commentary, edited by Charles F. Pfeiffer and Everett F. Harrison, Moody Press, 1962, p. 5.

ANIMALS CAN BE TRAINED

MAN CAN THINK

can do certain things that animals cannot do at all, for example, make things. It is true that animals can make nests or dams, but this is by instinct. When men build houses, bridges, computers or space ships, they invent and select. They think, reason, and create. Men are artists, but animals are not.

It is true that animals can "think"—that is, they can solve certain problems if confronted with the right set of circumstances and the need for something basic like food. But, as Adler observes, no animal "sits down to think" for the sake of thinking, as do engineers, educators or theologians.* And, no animal can communicate his thoughts. Animals may grunt, howl, whistle, whine, etc., but no animal can "talk with" another animal about what happened last week, or about a mechanism or situation that is not present.

The very fact that man is a "sinner" is evidence that he differs from animals in kind, not just degree. God intended man to be a "partner" with Him, someone with whom He could communicate. God also expected man to be responsible and obedient, but along with this requirement he gave man the freedom to choose to obey or disobey his Creator. Man can "determine his destiny" in a way that no animal could begin to even conceive.

For an evolutionist, such as Julian Huxley, to speculate that somewhere "way back there" a certain line of animals made an incredibly massive leap toward conceptual thought is interesting theory but hardly convincing fact. The findings of science, such as Dr. Leakey's "man ape fossils," do not void the Bible, nor do they "prove" organic evolution. Despite beautifully drawn time line charts such as in *Early Man* (Life Nature Library) the evolutionist (by his own admission) goes on a great deal of guesswork and supposition.

The evolutionist, who refuses to conceive of the supernatural as possible, has a right to his point of view, *but it is still only a point of view*. Evolutionists can point to "the findings of science" to prove their position, but the Christian can turn to science also and see that the complexities of all creation and especially life itself are infinitely beyond the element of chance or "natural selection."

*See **Ideas from the Great Books**, Mortimer J. Adler, Publisher's Hall Syndicate.

THE ROAD TO HOMO SAPIENS

God's Man Is Who I Am

A speck of cosmic dust—
A germ within a cell—
A cog to turn a wheel—
A link in a leaden chain—
Oh no, for I've the inexpressible joy
To scream—
    I am God's man!

Not a cosmic particle,
Nor an insignificant germ;
Not a mere mechanical cog,
Nor a lifeless leaden link!
Oh, no, for I can love and feel and think!
Yes, I must repeat—
    I am God's man!

They say I'm really ape-like,
A monkey running 'round;
They call it evolution—
One cell—some change—and man.
But oh, the special wonder
Of a God-created man—
    I am God's man!

I peel an orange
And taste its citric tartness—
I pick a jasmine blossom
And its fragrance fills my head.
I piece a poem together
And find my own expression—
I perceive complete fulfillment
In the one I'll find to love.
Impossible that I just happened,
Or developed bit by bit—
    I am God's man!

OR CREATED IN GOD'S IMAGE?

"And man became
    a living soul."
So says the Holy Book;
A universe of order,
A God of love, yet righteous,
A God-created Adam—
Oh, how I believe it—
    I am God's man!

By Sandra Wetther, **Journal of the American Scientific Affiliation,**
June, 1967.

Man's personality, mind and soul consciousness are so far above the animal's that even evolutionists are perplexed at this vast gulf.

The Christian admits that he does not know "scientifically" how God made man from the "dust of the earth" but then, the Bible is not a book of scientific explanations. The Bible's purpose is not to give details on *how* God made man, but *why* He made him. The Christian can look at God's Word and at all creation and say with confidence, "I am *God's* man!"

For further reading

Paperbacks

Darwin, Evolution, and Creation, Edited by Paul A. Zimmerman, Concordia Publishing House, 1959. See especially pp. 125-135.

The Case For Creation, Wayne Frair, P. William Davis, Moody Press, 1967. See chapter 5, "The Study of Man."

Hardbacks

Creation Revealed, F. A. Filby, Fleming H. Revell Company, 1964. See especially chapter 17 and 18 on the origin of man.

The Bible, Science and Creation, S. Maxwell Coder, George F. Howe, Moody Press, 1965. See especially chapter 8, "The Creation of Man."

Early Man, F. Clark Howell and the editors of *Life,* Life Nature Library, Time, Inc., 1965. A strictly evolutionist interpretation of the origin of man. The excellent full color drawings are a graphic example of how a theory can be made to look convincing by use of artist's reconstructions.

The Human Evolution, Ashley Montagu, World Publishing, 1965. Presents the standard arguments of the organic evolutionist in popular writing style. Dr. Montagu is the former head of the anthropology department of Rutgers University.

Periodicals

"The Naked Ape," Desmond Morris, *Life,* December 22, 1967. Morris' article is a good example of the kind of reasoning an organic evolutionist can use to "prove" his theory, although he has no real evidence for many of his statements.

CHAPTER 10

Does Genesis conflict with modern science?

There have been many conflicts between science and Christianity. Some of the most bitter disputes have to do with the "beginnings." Genesis means "the beginning" and the first eleven chapters of this first book of the Bible describe such things as the beginning of the universe, the sun and stars, the moon and earth, plant and animal life, and man.

In Genesis are the reports of Adam and Eve, Cain and Abel, long-lived patriarchs such as Methuselah, and Noah's Great Flood. All of these have been battlegrounds. And yet, once again, a lot of the conflict is only apparent. A lot of it springs from errors on both sides—faulty interpretations of Scripture colliding with unproved scientific theories. For example, there are philosophers and scientists who ridicule the Bible because they think it says the earth was created in six days, about 4,000 B.C.

Does the Bible teach that creation took place about 4,000 B.C.?

Many people, both Christian and anti-Christian, think so. But that's not the case. The date, 4,004 B.C., for creation was calculated by a seventeenth century archbishop named Ussher. Because he was an archbishop, people assumed that Ussher had to be right. So, for 300 years that date has appeared in the margins of many Bibles. Today's scientists laugh at the 4,004 B.C. date because their theories and findings point to a very old earth, possibly several billion years old.

But what does the Bible say? Simply: "In the beginning God created the heavens and earth." When was "the beginning"? The Bible doesn't say. "The beginning" could have been a few thousand years ago or it could have happened millions of years ago. So, is there a conflict between science and the Bible? No, the conflict is between certain theories of science and a certain theory of Archbishop Ussher.

What makes the first chapters of Genesis so important? What do they teach?

The first chapters of Genesis are above all a magnificent revelation from God that deals with the foundational relationships of the universe: the relationship of God to nature; of God to man; of man to nature; and of man to man. These chapters are also a foundation for the entire Bible. Every moral and spiritual law that follows is built solidly on this account of God's creative work.

For example, the Bible forbids idolatry because it means worship of the creature rather than the Creator. Murder is sinful because it is an assault on a creature made in the image of God. Man should not worship the stars and planets because they are only part of God's

140

creation.

The early chapters of Genesis also teach that man does not need to fear invisible powers, ghosts or demons, because God made all things, visible and invisible, and He is sovereign over all. Men should live as brothers because, black, white or yellow, all men are all of one blood, all of us have the same Creator. Divorce is against God's purpose in having man and woman become "one flesh" in marriage.

These are just a few examples. Look up some others for yourself in Genesis 1—11. Also look at the Ten Commandments, at the messages of the prophets, at the teachings of Jesus Christ. In each case, you will find that every moral and spiritual law is built on the Genesis account of creation.

Should Christians "write off" science because some scientists attack the Bible?

Christians cannot ignore scientific criticisms, unfair and ill-founded as some of these attacks may be. Some scientists may be agnostics and atheists, but science itself is an objective discipline that seeks truth wherever it may be found. The findings of science regarding the vastness of the universe and the intricate design of the earth and man himself all assure the Christian of God's sovereign creative power. But the Christian cannot ignore other scientific findings, for example the age of the earth and the dinosaur fossils, simply because these findings appear to be difficult to "reconcile with Scripture."

The Christian must proceed on the principle that God is creator of nature and therefore author of science, which is the study of nature. God is also author of Scripture. Therefore—ultimately—science and Scripture cannot conflict, although there may be apparently unsolvable contradictions at the present time.

Then just how does the Christian explain the "six days of creation" in Genesis 1?

The gap theory is one of the best known attempts by Christians to reconcile Scripture with the great age of the earth and the discoveries of fossils that show that dinosaurs once roamed the earth. The gap theory was developed by George H. Pember in the nineteenth century. The theory proposes that between Gen. 1:1 and Gen. 1:2 there may have been a period of indeterminate time—from thousands to millions of years—and that this period or "gap" could account for the vast ages that are reported in current geological findings.

Geologist Edwin K. Gedney says that the gap theorists would read the first two verses of Genesis as follows: "In the beginning, God created the heaven and the earth. And (after an indefinite period of time suitable for the geological ages) the earth became waste and empty."[*] The gap theorist's interpretation of the verse implies that the universe existed for possibly a great length of time and then at least the surface of the earth experienced a period of catastrophe in which most or all of its life perished. After the catastrophe, God recreated the earth in a period of six days of twenty-four hours each.

Other teachings in the gap theory include that during the indeterminate period between Gen. 1:1 and 2, the fall of the angels (II Peter 2:4; Jude 6) and the fall of Satan (Isa. 14:12-14) occurred. Gap theorists say Gen. 1:1 describes an original, perfect creation and Gen. 1:2 describes how this perfect creation was destroyed by God because of rebellion by Satan and the evil angels.

Although the gap theory has helped many Christians reconcile the geological record and the dinosaur fossils

[*]See "Geology and the Bible," by Edwin K. Gedney, **Modern Science and the Christian Faith,** Scripture Press, 1948, p. 47.

THE GAP THEORY

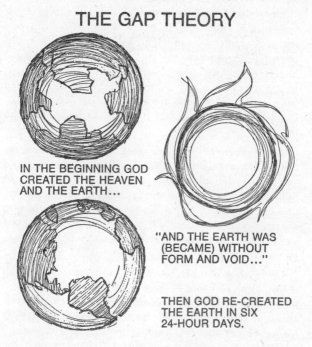

IN THE BEGINNING GOD
CREATED THE HEAVEN
AND THE EARTH...

"AND THE EARTH WAS
(BECAME) WITHOUT
FORM AND VOID..."

THEN GOD RE-CREATED
THE EARTH IN SIX
24-HOUR DAYS.

with Genesis 1:1-26, it has also left many questions in the minds of committed Christian scholars. Dr. C. I. Scofield *(The Scofield Reference Bible)* held to the gap theory and was instrumental in popularizing it. In a footnote on Gen. 1:2, Scofield says, "Jeremiah 4:23-26; Isaiah 24:1 and 45:18 clearly indicate that the earth had undergone a cataclysmic change as the result of divine judgement. The face of the earth bears everywhere the marks of such a catastrophe. There are not wanting intimations which connect it with a previous testing and fall of angels. See Ezekiel 28:12-15 and Isaiah 14:9-14, which certainly go beyond the kings of

Tyre and Babylon."*

However, *The New Scofield Reference Bible*, which was revised and republished in 1967, allows for two main interpretations of Gen. 1:1, 2. One is the gap theory. The other view is called an "original chaos" interpretation, which implies there is no break or "gap" between verses 1 and 2 and that the words "without form and void" in v. 2 are a description of an original formless matter in the first stage of the creation of the universe.**

Today many Christian scholars feel that the "original chaos" intepretation of Gen. 1:1, 2 is a more accurate view than the gap theory. These scholars point out difficulties in the gap theory on linguistic and geological grounds. Many Hebrew linguists point out that to interpret v. 2 as "the earth *became* without form and void" (instead of *was* without form and void) is inaccurate and forced.

Christian geologists see many problems in the gap theory also. To which "catastrophe" does the gap theory refer? The orderly progression of fossils in the rocks—a standard argument used by evolutionists for their theory of organic evolution—is unexplained. To many Christian scholars, the gap theory seems to read too much into the text that is not there.***

If the gap theory is not universally accepted, what are other interpretations of Genesis 1?

Flood geology is a different approach that explains the fossils in the rocks and the various geologic strata

*The Scofield Reference Bible, Oxford University Press, 1909, p. 3.
**The New Scofield Reference Bible, Oxford University Press, 1967, p. 1.
***For discussions of the gap theory, see Modern Science and the Christian Faith, Edwin Gedney, pp. 47, 49; Creation Revealed, F. A. Filby, Revell, pp. 55-58; The Christian View of Science and Scripture, Bernard Ramm, Eerdmans, pp. 195-210.

THE FLOOD THEORY SAYS

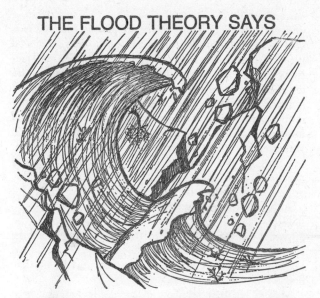

FOSSILS AND ROCK FORMATIONS ARE
DUE TO THE GENESIS CATASTROPHE

by claiming that all of these geological phenomena were
caused by the great flood described in Genesis 6–8.
Flood geologists claim that the six days of Genesis 1
were consecutive twenty-four hour periods occurring
some ten thousand years ago. Flood geology was popular during the eighteenth century, but was abandoned
during the nineteenth century in favor of long ages and
"uniformitarian" geology, which was proposed by Sir
Charles Lyell, the father of modern geological science.

During the twentieth century, however, there has
been a revival of flood geology, which started with the
teachings of George McCready Price, who wrote *The
New Geology* in 1923. Price took sharp issue with the
claims of uniformitarian geology which holds that the

various strata of the rocks have been deposited in a uniform, steady fashion over tremendously long periods of time, according to known physical and chemical laws. (Using equipment capable of measuring radioactivity in the rocks, the uniformitarian geologist dates the earth at over three billion years old.)

Flood geologists challenge the radioactive methods of dating and claim they are highly questionable and inaccurate. They maintain that the earth is much younger than three billion years and they account for the strata in the rocks and the fossils by saying that all of these were laid down through the catastrophic upheavals caused by the Genesis flood.

Although differing greatly from the gap theory, flood geology has the same appeals in that it accounts for the apparent geological record in the rocks. Flood geology also deals a fatal blow to the theory of evolution because it does not allow for the vast periods of time needed for the organic evolutionary process.

Many Christian scholars, however, including Christian geologists, seriously question the claims of flood geology and say that the mass of evidence for uniformitarian geology simply cannot be written off that easily. Christian geologists who hold to uniformitarian geology point to such evidence as the coal beds of the world, which appear to have been formed by successive growths of hundreds of feet of vegetation. Another standard piece of evidence is exposed rock strata, such as Specimen Ridge in Yellowstone Park, which shows how eighteen successive forests were wiped out by lava—apparently over a period of many thousands of years.

The principles of flood geology have been presented in recent years by Henry Morris, Ph.D., Professor and Head, Department of Civil Engineering, Virginia Polytechnic Institute and John C. Whitcomb, Jr., Ph.D., Professor of Old Testament, Grace Theological Seminary, Winona Lake, Indiana. In their book, *The Genesis Flood*, Morris and Whitcomb take sharp issue with all uniformitarian principles of geology and put forth their own explanations for the coal beds, Specimen Ridge in Yellowstone Park and other rock strata. Whitcomb and Morris maintain that all of these phenomena can be accounted for by a universal catastrophic deluge which they interpret as the Genesis flood, and which they believe included huge earthquakes and tidal waves rushing at thousands of miles an hour.*

The gap theory and flood geology both interpret the six days of creation as literal twenty-four hour days. However, those who see difficulties in the gap theory and flood geology, for reasons mentioned above, interpret the six days in another way, which they feel helps account for the geologic ages and the fossils.

Are the six days of Genesis 1 ever interpreted as other than 24-hour periods?

The day-age theory is based on the view that the Hebrew word *yom* in Genesis 1, which is translated as "day," can also be properly translated as "time" or "age." Raymond F. Surburg observes that *yom* occurs some 1,480 times in the Old Testament and it can be translated by fifty different words, such as "life" and "forever" in addition to words like "day" or "time."

Surburg points out that *yom* is used in three different ways in Gen. 1:1—2:4. In Gen. 1:5 the word "day" is used to refer to the light part of the day (in contrast to night) as well as a certain period of time—"one day." In Gen. 2:4, "day" is obviously used to refer to all six "days" of Genesis 1. Day-age theorists conclude that there is really no way of telling from the context of

---

*The Genesis Flood, John C. Whitcomb, Jr., and Henry Morris, Presbyterian and Reformed Publishing Company, 1961. See especially chapters 4-7.

Gen. 1:1—2:4 how long a period is meant by *yom.**

A paragraph in *The New Scofield Reference Bible* points out that the terms evening and morning may be limited to mean a "solar day" but the frequent parabolic use of natural phenomena may warrant the conclusion that it simply means that each creative day was a period of time marked off by a beginning and ending . . . in any event the sun did not become a measure of time before the fourth day, as seen in vs. 14-18.**

The six days of creation, say the day-age theorists, roughly correspond to the vast periods of geologic time and point to stages of "Progressive creation" rather than six literal days of creation. Therefore, a holder of the day-age theory can accept the age of the earth according to the estimates of the geological time table which stretch back as far as several billion years.

In opposition to the day-age theory, Raymond Surburg criticizes the interpretation of *yom* as a long period of time by pointing out that:

(1) A well established hermeneutical principle is that the student of Scripture should stick to the original and literal meaning of a word unless there is a compelling reason for adopting a figurative or derived interpretation. Surburg feels there is no reason for a figurative interpretation in Genesis 1.

(2) Surburg claims that most reputable Hebrew dictionaries do not recognize or allow the interpretation as "a period of time" to be understood as lasting millions of years.

(3) In the Old Testament when the word *yom* is associated with a definite numeral, solar days are meant. Surburg cites Gen. 7:11; 8:14; 17:12 and Exod. 12:6 for examples.

*See **Darwin, Evolution and Creation**, edited by Paul F. Zimmerman, Concordia Publishing House, 1959, p. 59.
**The New Scofield Reference Bible, Oxford University Press, 1967, p. 2.

(4) The wording of Genesis 1 seems to indicate a short time for the creative acts described. There is no hint at eons of time. But instantaneous action seems to be stressed.

(5) Surburg also charges that interpreting *yom* as a long period of time fails to bring about the desired harmony between evolution and the Bible. According to Surburg, geology does not teach the evolution of the world in six geological epochs, nor does the order of events in Genesis conform to those of the evolutionary scheme.*

What is the "right" interpretation of Genesis 1?

Should the Christian be embarrassed because he can't give an absolute answer to this question? Not at all. Scientists have the same kinds of problems. For example: what is light? Is it waves or is it particles? The evidence is contradictory. Sometimes it seems to be one thing, sometimes another. Most scientists simply don't know. According to Sir William Bragg, "We teach quantum (particle) theory on Mondays, Wednesdays and Fridays, and wave theory on Tuesdays, Thursdays and Saturdays."** In other words scientists have evidence that needs an adequate theory to explain it. So far as Genesis 1 is concerned, the Christian may see himself in a similar position.

Sincere Christians may hold different opinions about the precise meanings of certain words in Genesis 1 or the length of time involved in creation. But all Christians agree on the great theological truths contained in the first chapter of the Bible.

Christians agree that Genesis 1 establishes that *the*

*See **Darwin, Evolution and Creation**, pp. 59, 60. Dr. Surburg, Professor of Theology, Concordia Teachers College, is one of four authors of **Darwin, Evolution and Creation**.
See **Science Is a Sacred Cow, Anthony Standen, E. P. Dutton, 1950, Dutton paperback edition, p. 68.

God of the Bible is the God of creation. In simple, straightforward language Genesis tells us what we really need to know: *God made the universe. God made all living things. God made us.*

Obviously the Genesis 1 account is not written in scientific language. This actually is one of the chief marks of its divine inspiration. If it had been written in the scientific language of our day it would have been unintelligible to the people of Bible times and it would most certainly be outdated and inaccurate a century from now.* The Bible was written for all men everywhere—for men of every century.

It all comes down to this: the Bible doesn't claim to be a scientific account, but it cannot be proved unscientific. The Bible plainly teaches that God created the heaven and the earth, but it gives no scientific specifics. It cannot be proved or disproved according to current scientific evidence. As one Bible scholar points out, there is no way to turn back the clock to the beginning. The subject lies beyond the scope and abilities of natural science.**

While man's inquiring mind strives to match the Genesis creation account with evidence from his world, the fact remains that God's Spirit did not direct Moses to explain just how God used time in accomplishing creation. Why is it necessary to reduce the greatness of the Genesis account of creation to scientific terms?

Christians should be open to ideas of science and not get panicky every time a new discovery is announced. And Christians should be open to interpretations of the Bible, but not necessarily committed to these interpretations to the point where faith and personal trust in

*The New Bible Commentary, edited by F. Davidson, Wm. B. Eerdmans Publishing Co., p. 76.
**See The Way, the Truth and the Life, John R. Lavik, Augsburg Publishing House, 1957, p. 37.

150

GENESIS I TELLS WHO NOT HOW

Jesus Christ depends on a certain interpretation.

Centuries ago, Augustine gave some excellent advice to the effect that we should not rush headlong to one opinion or the other, because there is always the possibility that a hastily adopted viewpoint can turn out to be false, and if our faith is dependent on that view it can appear false, too. And we will be arguing for our own opinions rather than the real doctrines of Scripture.*

*The above is a paraphrase of Augustine's words in **De Genesi ad Litteram**. The statement is quoted in full in **Modern Science and the Christian Faith**, Scripture Press, 1950, p. 57.

For further reading

Paperbacks

The Bible and Modern Science, Henry M. Morris, Moody Press, 1951. See especially chapter 3 on "Modern Science and the Flood." Dr. Morris is a convinced holder of the flood geology theory.

Science Speaks, Peter W. Stoner, Moody Press, 1958. See especially Dr. Stoner's comments on the six days of Genesis, pp. 68-72.

Darwin, Evolution and Creation, edited by Paul A. Zimmerman, Concordia Publishing House, 1959. See especially chapter 2 "In the Beginning God Created," by Raymond F. Surburg. All of the various interpretations of Genesis 1 are discussed.

The Case for Creation, Wayne Frair, P. William Davis, Moody Press, 1967. See chapter 6, "The Bible and Creation."

Hardbacks

The Genesis Flood, John C. Whitcomb, Henry M. Morris, The Presbyterian and Reformed Publishing Company, 1961. A detailed presentation in defense of the theory of flood geology.

The Christian View of Science and Scripture, Bernard Ramm, William B. Eerdmans Publishing Company, 1955. See especially chapter 6 on geology which deals with various theories of creation and the six days of Genesis. Dr. Ramm covers all the basic interpretations and gives their strengths and weaknesses as he sees them.

Is There A Conflict Between Genesis 1 and Natural Science? N. H. Ridderbos, William B. Eerdmans Publishing Company, 1957. A brief but thorough study of Genesis 1 and its relationship to modern science.

CHAPTER 11

Is science a sacred cow?

Science is pretty impressive stuff. Einstein said that matter could be changed into energy, and the scientists went ahead and made an atomic bomb. From science and technology we have received some marvelous benefits, all the way from television to penicillin. And there is every reason to expect these benefits to keep coming. Kidney and heart transplants today, cancer may be cured tomorrow, and the day after, scientists might come up with a way to feed all the hungry millions in the world. Science is useful. That's one of the reasons we find it so interesting.

How does science work? What's it all about? The main technique of science—the way things are discovered—is what is called "the Scientific Method." Barrels of ink have been spent defining this method, but here is an attempt to sum it up in a few words.

First of all, there is observation, often done as a carefully planned experiment. After a number of observations are collected, the scientist forms a hypothesis (a suggested explanation of what he has observed).

Next, the scientist says, "If my hypothesis is true, then when I do such and such an experiment, so and so ought to happen." The final step is to do the experiment. If it turns out different than expected, the hypothesis falls. If the experiment works, the hypothesis is temporarily accepted.

But there is more. Other experiments are done. If the hypothesis survives every test, it is promoted. It now becomes a "theory." A theory is a bit more solid than a hypothesis, but theories can also be shot down.

Back in the early days of physics, everyone believed in a substance called "the luminiferous aether" or "ether," for short (not, of course, the chemical ether used in medicine). According to the theory, "ether" could not be seen, felt, tasted, measured or weighed. Yet it was supposed to be everywhere, filling all space and all matter.

The great physicist, Lord Kelvin, stated that he was just as positive that "ether" existed as he was of anything. Today's physicists aren't quite so positive. In fact, after having been believed for about a century, the theory of "luminiferous aether" collapsed with a dull thud. Nobody talks about it today except as a joke. So even the best established of scientific theories can be upset.

The perfect example of forgetting that scientific theory may be upset at any time is the belief of many scientists in Darwin's theory of organic evolution. Evolution has been "proved" in that scientists have observed micro-(small change) evolution within certain species. But micro-evolution does not prove macro-(amoeba-to-man) evolution.

Scientists have experimented, but they've never yet been able to produce macro-evolution under laboratory conditions. They have, for example, bred thousands and thousands of generations of Drosophila (banana flies). They have bred flies with red eyes, short wings, hairless, dwarfed, stunted, and in other ways so changed as to be hardly flies at all. Yet they have never managed to "evolute" Drosophila into anything else but a banana fly.

What's the difference between science and "scientism"?

The sudden prominence of science in the nineteenth century spawned a philosophy called "scientism." This concept (which swept the Western world) inferred that science could solve all problems and bring perfect happiness to mankind. As a result, belief in God and the Bible were thought to be unnecessary; in fact, religion was even considered an obstacle to scientific progress.

But science and scientism are two different things. The definition of science is "to know," "to understand." The scientist makes observations and confines his reports to findings dealing with time, space and matter. In many cases, he supplements his sense organs with instruments.* Yet, his responsibility is still to *report*, not to *interpret*. Others take these facts and interpret them according to the world view they accept. Whether scientific discoveries are good or bad depends on the one who decides what to do with them.

In its most extreme form, scientism is the worship of scientific achievement with the purpose of ruling God out of human life. Organic evolution can become a form of scientism, when it is used as a foundation for a philosophical system that serves as a self-sufficient key to the universe and as a basis for ethical decisions.

Elving Anderson, writing in the *Journal of the American Scientific Affiliation*, finds it helpful to refer

*See Modern Science and the Christian Life, John W. Klotz, Concordia, 1961, pp. 54, 55.

to this viewpoint as "evolutionism" or a form of scientism. He points out that the evolutionary humanism expounded by Julian Huxley is clearly opposed to faith in the Bible and Christ, and that Huxley is preaching his personal religion, not teaching as a scientist.[*]

Have religion and theology been affected by evolutionism?

In *Science Is a Sacred Cow*, Anthony Standen refers to a point made by philosopher G. K. Chesterton, who observed that evolution's popularity from the time of Darwin until now is not solely because of its scientific value. The implications in the theory of organic evolution involve morals and human behavior. The important point is whether God "interferes," as it were, with what happens on this earth (creationism); or whether He leaves it alone or never had anything to do with it in the first place (organic evolution).[**] Today the effects of evolutionism can be seen in every segment of human society, including religion and theology.

Religion and theology were affected because many theologians, fully understanding the implications of the evolutionistic theory, concluded that the whole Bible was full of the mistakes of people evolving from pagan polytheism to monotheism. Higher criticism of the Scriptures became the order of the day. The Biblical history of Israel was reinterpreted by religious thinkers who had accepted the evolutionary point of view. These effects of evolutionism led to liberalism, neo-orthodoxy and modern existentialism, all of which have a low view of Scripture and a high view of man's interpretation of Scripture.

[*] See "The Goals of the American Scientific Affiliation: A Personal View," V. Elving Anderson, **Journal of the American Scientific Affiliation**, June 1965, p. 34.
[**] See Science Is a Sacred Cow, Anthony Standen, E. P. Dutton and Company, p. 28.

Has evolutionism influenced philosophy and education?

John Dewey, the most influential educational philosopher of our century, based much of his thinking on ideas behind Darwin's theory. Dewey had no place for God in his structure. He stressed man's experience and man's ability to grow and change.

Progressive education, which was built on Dewey's ideas, generally ignores or plays down the supernatural and the teachings of the Bible and is concerned primarily with an individual's "secular" growth.

Has evolutionism affected sociology and psychology? (Is the "new morality" really new?)

Mortimer Adler, the philosopher who heads Chicago's Institute for Philosophic Research, points out that to believe that man is not basically different from animals actually undermines all humanity. One of the foundations of society is that all human beings are equal in their humanity and should be treated equally, not discriminated against.

Adler suggests that evolutionism opens the way to Hitler's doctrine that "there is a greater difference between the lowest forms still called human and our superior races than between the lowest man and monkeys of the highest order."

Adler believes that the image we hold of man is crucial because it directly affects how we will treat each other. As far as he is concerned, man is unique, not a brute, not a machine.*

In the area of ethics and morals, evolutionism's effect can be seen in what is called today "the new morality." If man is evolving according to the forces of blind

*The Difference of Man and the Difference It Makes, Mortimer J. Adler, Holt, Rinehart and Winston, 1967.

157

chance and natural selection, it follows that there are no absolute standards of right and wrong. For the evolutionist, ethics and morals are relative.

Evolutionism also affected the field of psychology. For example, evolutionistic principles are behind the thinking of Sigmund Freud, who based his theories of personality on the idea that man is nothing more than a higher type of animal, different in degree and not in kind.

Evolutionism is the primary example of how scientism emphasizes human reason and human intellect. Scientism assumes powers it does not have. It creates dogmas to offer "explanations" for the world and for man's place in the world. Scientism has exaggerated ideas about what science can do and considers science a universal cure-all for mankind.

Scientism fails to see that science has many important limitations. Scientism lives under the delusion that science is infallible and beyond criticism. As one scientist has pointed out, scientism has made science the great "sacred cow" of our time.*

Why has there been conflict between the Bible and science?

The first great debate between theologians and scientists happened about 400 years ago. It concerned the theories of Copernicus. Copernicus taught that the planets revolved around the sun. A bit later, Galileo constructed a telescope, looked into the heavens and announced that Copernicus was right. But the Roman Catholic Church didn't receive this very happily.

The church proclaimed: "The proposition that the sun is the center of the world and immovable from its place is absurd, philosophically false, and formally

*Science Is a Sacred Cow, Anthony Standen, p. 34.

heretical; it is expressly contrary to the Holy Scripture." The Scripture that church fathers had in mind was Psalm 104:5, "Who laid the foundations of the earth that it should not be removed forever."

Galileo was forced to recant on his knees and say that the earth doesn't move.* But even though the church "won," people gradually came to see that Galileo was right, and Christians came to see that the Copernican theory was not opposed to Psalm 104:5. The first so-called "conflict" between the Bible and science was really a case of scientific theory versus a certain interpretation of Scripture.

What about Darwin's theory and the Bible?

This "biggest battle" between theologians and scientists is still going on. The first shots were fired by Samuel Wilberforce and Thomas Henry Huxley on the evening of June 30, 1860 about a year after Darwin's publication of *The Origin of Species*.

The Huxley-Wilberforce debate came about like this: Thomas Huxley was thirty-six years old, a professor of natural history and paleontology at the Government School of Mines in London. He was a well-known lecturer and an author and definitely "on the way up" in British scientific circles. But Huxley began criticizing some of the views held by Richard Owen, the most famous English biologist of the day. On one occasion, Huxley humiliated Owen before the Royal Society by pointing out several serious errors in a paper Owen had written on comparative anatomy.

A little later Huxley came out with praise for Darwin's recently published book, *The Origin of Species*. Owen attacked Huxley anonymously concerning Hux-

*As Galileo got up, he supposedly muttered to himself, "But it does move." See "Science v. Theology; The Battle Isn't Over Yet," Bernard Ramm, Eternity magazine, October 1965, p. 17.

ley's views on the book. A battle began shaping up and Owen decided that he would get Samuel Wilberforce, Bishop of Oxford, to oppose Huxley in a debate on Darwin's theory of organic evolution by natural selection.

Wilberforce was a brilliant debater and Owen was sure that, by giving the Bishop some coaching on biology, he could humiliate Huxley and gain revenge on his rival.

Wilberforce was eager to debate Huxley in order to bolster his sagging prestige and to build himself up as a "champion of orthodox Christianity." But, brilliant as he was, Wilberforce was not a trained scientist. The few hours of preparation he had with Owen's help, were not enough to prevent him from making several careless and erroneous statements, which Huxley was quick to point out. Worst of all, in his conclusion, Wilberforce sarcastically asked whether Huxley claimed descent from monkeys on his mother's side, an obvious appeal to the Victorian prejudice of the day that made women "angels".*

Huxley's reply was shattering: "I would rather be descended from a poor chattering ape than from a man of great talents who would appeal to prejudice rather than to truth."

Wilberforce was finished. So was any possibility of presenting orthodox Christianity to the scientists of that day, because they believed Wilberforce's claim to speak for orthodox Christianity. From then on, as far as many scientists were concerned, orthodoxy was associated with prejudice, ignorance, error, egotism, and opposition to science. This breakdown in communication between theologians and scientists has not been fully

---

*A metaphorical term used to describe women of the nineteenth century as "angelic", without fault or blemish in character.

overcome even to this day. Many scientists still distrust religion and, unfortunately, have consciously (or unconsciously) turned to scientism as a substitute for belief in the God who created the universe.*

How can the Christian answer someone who has a philosophy of life based on scientism?

Physics professor Allen Moen points to Job chapter 38 as one example of God's answer to scientism, the philosophy that denies the God of the Bible and worships man's scientific achievements instead.

The book of Job, of course, tells how Job trusted God even while he was being severely tested. Several of Job's friends come to see him and try to explain the reason for his suffering. They argue that his sufferings must be the result of sin, guilt, hypocrisy, and lying. Job denies their charges and claims innocence, righteousness and a clean heart. But even though Job shows insight concerning God's moral requirements, he also shows self-righteousness, something which is at the root of pride, and idolatry.

In chapter 38 God begins to nudge Job off his pedestal of self-righteousness. He asks, "Who are you, Job? You think you have all the answers but you don't. Where were you when I created the earth?" (See Job 38:1.4.) God goes on to ask Job other questions for which Job has no answer. The whole point is to show Job he is the creature, God is the Creator and man has no right to self-righteousness and pride.

Would today's scientist be humbled by God's words to Job? Not necessarily. Through modern science we know the answers to many of the questions that God

*For an excellent account of the Wilberforce-Huxley debate, see "The Conflict between Christianity and Biological Science," David F. Siemens, Journal of the American Scientific Affiliation, March 1966, p. 5.

asked of Job. Undoubtedly we will know more. We know where snow and hail are stored. We know where light and darkness come from. We know how wide the earth is. We even have information on how the earth was formed.

As Physics professor Allen Moen observes, some of the questions God asks of Job seem almost naive when compared to modern man's vast knowledge of the universe.

But, asks Moen, suppose God were writing to a modern Job? Some of his questions might sound like this:

Where were you when I first filled the center of space with neutrons?
   Tell me if you have understanding.
Who decided the half-life of neutron-decay, that led to electrons and protons and the buildup of the elements?
Or was that the way the foundations were laid? Do you know?
Where does matter get its mass-energy with which it can resist acceleration, and why does it resist acceleration?
   Tell me, oh modern man, you who have worked with accelerators and measured the effect numberless times.
Where is the way to the dwelling of cosmic rays, and where do the elusive neutrinoes go?
What is in a brain that produces thought? Now you claim that its RNA molecules chemically record all its sensations, the secret of memory is at your fingertips.
But, oh modern man, where do your thoughts lie—in the brain, too? Bring me a thought that we may examine it.*

Moen makes his point well. Man has discovered scientific truths and laws. By putting these laws to work he is able to conquer disease, span continents in supersonic transports in a few hours, probe outer space

*From "Some Limitations of Science," Allen L. Moen, **Church Herald**, Oct. 7, 1966, p. 4.

162

and schedule a landing on the moon for the 1970's, perhaps before.

But, no matter how many scientific truths man discovers, he still faces countless questions, some of which he will never be able to answer. In addition, some of the answers that man has decided on are tentative and subject to change at any moment.

Dr. Vannevar Bush, honorary board chairman of Massachusetts Institute of Technology and recognized as the father of the modern analogue computer, says, "Science never proves anything in an absolute sense." He adds, "Science, when understood properly, makes man humble in his ignorance and smallness. Man will follow science where it leads, but not where it cannot lead. And with a pause, he will admit a faith."*

As Alfred Wong, Professor of Physics, U.C.L.A. points out: "Science enables man to understand and appreciate the creation around him. Through science, man's limitations are set forth. The Bible, on the other hand, is divine revelation, giving an authoritative and unified account about the Creator and the origin in creation which science seldom dwells upon. To a believer, science serves to reveal the wonderful details in creation and yet at the same time humbles man by reminding him how imperfect still is his knowledge. The scientific ability is one of the many gifts of God given to us so that we might join the Psalmist in proclaiming the Heavens are telling the Glory of God; and the firmament proclaims his handiwork."

What is the relationship of science and Scripture?

God has revealed himself in both nature and in His Word. The Bible is the revelation of God. Science is

*See **Time**, May 7, 1965, p. 81.

the study of nature. The purposes of science and the purposes of Scripture are different.

Psalm 19:1-6 is the revelation of God in nature. Nature shows evidence of a Creator. There is order and design in nature. This by itself does not *prove* the existence of God, but it is certainly evidence of His existence and what He is like.

God's *written* revelation gives us a much more specific and exact knowledge (Psalm 19:7-14). The first part of Psalm 19 speaks of the "book of nature" and the second part tells us of the "book of the law" (the Bible).

How can we learn the most from these two books that God has written in nature and Scripture? With Job, we can realize that we are the created, not creators. We are fallible—and sinful.

There are two basic attitudes that man can hold toward God, as He is revealed in the Bible. Man can acknowledge God as his Creator, be humble, teachable. Or, man can go his own way. He can rebel. He can disavow God, even proclaim that God is dead.

The "Parable of the White Rat" illustrates the attitude of scientism quite well:

One day a scientist who was experimenting with white rats created an intricate maze, and in it he placed one of his choice white rats named "Theo" (short for "Theologian").

For days and weeks Theo was puzzled about the mysteries of the scientist's creation. He said to the other white rats in the laboratory, "How great is our scientist!"

Then one day, after weeks of experimenting, Theo was able to solve the baffling network of the maze.

With an air of arrogance, he turned to the other white rats in the laboratory and said, "Our scientist is dead."*

Dr. James Shaw, biological chemist, pinpoints the

*Ray E. Stahl, Director of Information, Milligan College, in Christianity Today, Nov. 24, 1967.

limitations of science and the dead end of making science a sacred cow with this observation:

"No standard for morals, no universal concern for one's neighbor, no satisfaction for the yearning human heart can spring from any amoral, impersonal body of knowledge. Science has no answer to man's dilemma. Science can never displace Jehovah God of the Bible as Lawgiver and Jesus Christ His Son as Savior and mediator between God and sinful man."[*]

For Further Reading

Paperbacks

Modern Science in the Christian Life, John W. Klotz, Concordia Publishing House, 1961. A rational and readable explanation of the relationship between the Christian faith and modern science. Note chapters 3 and 4, "The Modus Operandi of Science," and "Science and the Supernatural."

Science Is a Sacred Cow, Anthony Standen, Dutton Paperbacks, E. P. Dutton and Company, Inc., 1950. Born in England, Anthony Standen was graduated from Oxford with honors in chemistry and then earned a degree in chemical engineering at Massachusetts Institute of Technology. Standen pokes holes in the presumptions and pomp of scientism with precision and humor.

Religion Without Revelation, Julian Huxley, Mentor Paperbacks, New American Library, 1958. The agnostic and humanist point of view by one of the most outspoken neo-Darwinists of the 20th century. Among Huxley's claims is the assertion that the idea of God has now become "an inadequate hypothesis." Huxley should be read as a graphic example of the anti-supernatural point of view.

For additional material, see "For Further Reading," chapter 12, p. 179, 180.

[*]See "What Some Scientists Say about God and the Supernatural," **Christianity Today**, Aug. 27, 1965. This article gives the views of some 30 men in all fields of science and from various countries, who agree that faith in Jesus Christ and His Gospel is the necessary axis for life that is truly life.

Can you be a scientific Christian?

"Scientific Christian"? What does that mean?

Let's reword the question and put it this way: Can a Christian operate effectively in today's space age where science and technology reign supreme, or is Christianity really for the little old ladies and little kids?

Many critics of the Bible and the church believe it's the latter—that Christians are hopelessly childish, behind the times and just plain "out of it." In addition they assert or imply that Christianity is "anti-scientific" and that the church has hampered and opposed scientific progress for centuries. Are the "science-centered" critics right? To find the answer, why not use true scientific method: examine the evidence and see for yourself . . .

Should a Christian be science's friend? enemy? neutral?

Certainly the Christian should not be "an enemy of

science." The field of science, perhaps more than any other field, needs dedicated devoted Christian men and women. Since people respect scientists so highly, Christians who are scientists can command great respect as they witness for their faith.

Yet the Christian must try to keep things in focus. Wonderful as science is, only Scripture can tell us why we are here. Look, for example, at Psalm 8:3-6. Here we find the answers to some basic questions. What is man? Man is a creation of God, and he is crowned with God's glory and honor. *Why* is man? That is, what is his purpose? Psalm 8:6 says that God has put man in charge of all things on earth. Man is to "subdue the earth" (see Genesis 1:26-31). Most Christians who are scientists believe that this is authority from God to explore the wonders of creation and find ways to improve man's life on earth.

Will science "play God" through genetic control?

Genetic control of life is a much discussed subject. *Life* magazine and others have carried stories about scientists trying to manipulate genes to change the nature of man. Of course, much of this new knowledge is clearly beneficial. There have been advances against genetic diseases that were formerly incurable. Genes can be modified through medical treatment and perhaps sometime it will be possible to change the genes themselves. There are several ways this might take place. One method for gene changing is the technique of transformation. A quantity of bone marrow cells might be removed from a person afflicted with a genetic disease. DNA (the molecule that is the mechanism of life) from a normal person would be added. Eventually, the cells would be returned to the person's body so that the previous genetic deficiency would be

167

overcome by the action of the newly incorporated DNA.*

Genetic control is like atomic energy. It has enormous potential for good and equal potential for evil. Already, serious questions have been raised in the law courts that our present laws and social customs have been unable to cope with effectively. In addition, there is much talk of breeding a race of "supermen" through genetic surgery. Questions then arise as to what "qualities" are most desirable for a "superman" and what the supermen would do with the rest of us once they became numerous.

Successful transplants of human hearts have already been achieved and scientists are working on accomplishing a similar feat with the brain.** But when you transplant the new brain into a man, do you tamper with his soul? Is he then a "new person"?

As *Life* science editor Albert Rosenfeld has observed, the speed of scientific advancement and the changes occurring almost yearly will inevitably raise profound theological, ethical and moral questions.*** Is man ready or able to cope with his own scientific genius?

Without God and the moral absolutes of the Bible, man faces a perilous and unknown path. As never before, Christians are needed in these rapidly expanding scientific fields, so they can influence the use of man's knowledge, which has far outstripped his moral abilities and understanding.

*See "The Control of Man's Genetic Future," V. Elving Anderson, Journal of the American Scientific Affiliation, December 1966, p. 97. Dr. Anderson, Assistant Director of the Dight Institute for Human Genetics, University of Minnesota, points out that it is not a question of when genetic control will take place, but how it will be done. In fact, certain kinds of genetic control are already being used.
**See "The Dead Body and the Living Brain," Oriana Fallaci, Look, November 28, 1967, pp. 99.
***See "The New Man—What Will He Be Like?" Life Educational Reprint 32, reprinted from Life, October 1, 1965.

Is it true that Christianity has tried to delay scientific progress?

Because of all the battles between scientists and theologians, this might seem to be the case. But David F. Siemens, instructor at Los Angeles Pierce College, has traced the origins of science, and the evidence shows that modern science is the "offspring" of Christianity.*

As Siemens points out, why didn't the Greeks, for example, develop modern science? They certainly had the thinkers to do it. The Pythagoreans discovered the laws of harmony and the vibration of strings. Plato was a genius and a first rate mathematician. Aristotle developed logic and collected many facts. Euclid produced geometry. Other great thinkers were Archimedes, Appolonius of Perga, Nichomacus of Gerasa. Yet with all this logical and mathematical ability, the Greeks never developed any empirical (modern experimental) science. Why not?

The basic fallacy was their understanding of God. Plato's God was a craftsman, not a Creator. God was a workman who had to do the best he could with what was available. But things would never work out exactly. There were always tolerances, plusses and minuses. So Plato said that one cannot have a science of *things*, only of ideas. In other words, what we call "the real world" could not be understood.

Aristotle, who followed Plato, and who became *"the Philosopher"* of the later Middle Ages, did not even have a Creator-God. Aristotle's God was the ultimate Form that reacted against matter and thus produced everything in the world. Aristotle taught: There is no

*See "The Sources of Science," David F. Siemens, Jr., **Journal of the American Scientific Affiliation,** Sept., 1966, p. 84. Much of the material in this chapter is found in Mr. Siemens' carefully documented writings.

use trying to understand things; they cannot be understood because they have a meaningless core.

The Greek atomists, who have been given credit by some for beginning a sort of science, were no better off. Heraclitus believed that all things are in a perpetual state of flux, so that no knowledge of them is possible.

No one is foolish enough to seek order where they are sure that there is only disorder or illusion. This is why the Greeks never studied nature in a way that would lead to modern science. Certainly they had part of the answer. They had mathematics and logic. But something more is necessary for real science. There must be a belief that the world is rational and orderly. Where did this idea come from?

It came from Genesis 1:1: "In the beginning God created the heaven and the earth." And from Ephesians 1:11, where Paul speaks of God ". . . who worketh all things after the counsel of his own will." The Christian believes that the world is orderly because it was created by a rational God, a God of wisdom and truth.

From the Bible, Christians also came to believe that man is rational, in the same way that God is rational (although in a more limited way), for man was created in the image and likeness of God. Therefore man can think God's thoughts after Him. This is the motivating force behind science. Alfred North Whitehead, the noted philosopher, spoke of this belief in order:

"Without this belief, the incredible labors of scientists would be without hope. It is . . . the motive power of research—that there is a secret, a secret which can be revealed. When we compare this tone of thought in Europe with the attitude of other civilizations when left to themselves, there seems but one source for its origin. It must come from the medieval insistence on the rationality of God, conceived as with the personal energy of Jehovah and with the rationality of a Greek philosopher. Every detail was supervised and

170

ordered: the search into nature could only result in the vindication of the faith in rationality."*

It is a matter of record that science never developed anywhere except where there was Christian influence. In addition, the extension of science has come mainly in areas where the Bible was most freely read.

Galileo, one of the first of modern scientists, believed that he was "thinking God's thoughts after Him." Galileo wrote:

"As to the truth, of which mathematical demonstrations give us the knowledge, it is the same which the Divine Wisdom knoweth; but . . . the manner whereby God knoweth the infinite propositions, whereof we understand some few, is highly more excellent than ours . . ."**

Galileo's faith in a rational universe to which mathematics can be applied is still a basic premise of modern science. Certainly there are those scientists who deny that the universe is rationally organized. But even these men act as if the universe can be understood. They go on making discoveries, but they can give no explanation as to why we should be able to understand things.

Indeed, they become a little ridiculous, for their basic belief, shorn of big words and complicated phrases, is: The universe is orderly because I am orderly; the universe is understandable because I make it understandable.

It's a paradoxical fact: although many scientists (as well as followers of scientism) oppose Christianity and accuse Christians of being behind the times, science itself continues to bear the marks of its Christian origin. Indeed to remove the Christian parts of science would mean that there could be no science.

*Science and the Modern World, Alfred North Whitehead, Macmillan Company, 1948, p. 18. Quoted in "The Sources of Science," David F. Siemens, Journal of the ASA, September 1966, p. 85.
**Galileo, Letter to the Grand Duchess Christina in Stillman Drake, Discoveries and Opinions of Galileo, Doubleday Anchor Books, 1957. Quoted in "Sources of Science," Journal of the ASA, September, 1966.

Has science outgrown Christianity and made faith in God irrelevant?

The Bible is the revelation of God, written by men inspired by God. Science is a study of natural phenomena. In their efforts to harmonize (or widen the split between) the two, scientists and Christians have forgotten an essential fact: the purposes of science and the purposes of Scripture are different. The plain truth is that the Bible does not have to "match" science. To attempt to interpret Scripture to "match the findings of science" is to do injustice to science and the Bible.

Much of the strife, in fact, between science and the church during the past few centuries can be traced to the church's effort to try to match its interpretations of Scripture to the science of the current day. The church often looked like it was playing "catch-up" and that it was always at least a century or two behind science. When scientists junked one theory and proposed a more advanced one, many in the church opposed the new views in order to save face or to escape the problem of trying to "interpret the Bible to match the new findings."

Science has enjoyed fantastic growth—especially in the last few decades—and more triumphs and accomplishments surely lie ahead. It seems as though the child (science) has outgrown its parent (Christianity). It would do well for Christians today to avoid the trap of getting off firm theological ground to go out and duel with science about the accuracy of Scripture.

Science has not "outgrown God." Science is the product of the creature, not the Creator and scientists need God's eternal truth. Science is completely unable to answer the basic question: Who or what caused this universe, this earth and living things? The answer comes from the Psalmist, "The heavens declare the

In the 17th century, science was Christianity's "child," using basic Christian concepts of a rational universe and enjoying its greatest growth in countries where the Bible was taught and believed . . .

glory of God . . ." (Psalm 19:1). Scientists do well to ponder another question: What is man that God is mindful of him? The answer: God is mindful of man because He created man and gave him dominion over all the earth. (See Psalm 8:3-6.)

Nature is the first step in revelation, but God's written revelation gives us a still better view and more excellent knowledge (Psalm 19:7-14). While the first part of Psalm 19 speaks of the "book of nature" the second part tells us of God's book of the law (Scripture). And how can we learn the most from both of God's books? By keeping the right attitude, by being humble and teachable, and by avoiding sins of presumption, such as worshiping idols we make ourselves in our laboratories or on our production lines. As the

in the 20th century, although scientists still base their thinking on a rational universe and although scientists practice many virtues that are basically Christian, many scientists imply or openly claim that science has outgrown and surpassed Christian beliefs in a creator God ...

Psalmist says, "May my spoken words and unspoken thoughts be pleasing even to You, O Lord, my Rock and my Redeemer" (Psalm 19:14, *Living Psalms*).

How then is the Christian to operate in a scientific world?

First, the Christian should not be an "enemy of science." Nor should the Christian decide that since scientists aren't "so high and mighty after all" that he will now become disdainful and disrespectful of science. One of the tragedies of our day is that too many capable Christians have been driven from the ranks of science by an anti-scientific attitude fostered by fear and suspicion. The field of science, perhaps more than any other field, needs dedicated, devoted Christian men and women. Science needs the witness of Christians who will claim openly and unashamedly

174

I cannot understand how you can bother with mere puny man, to pay any attention to him: And yet... you have put him in charge of everything you made; everything is put under his authority.

Except for one thing . . .

that the basis for man's knowledge goes beyond scientific data and achievements to God, the Creator of the very materials with which the scientist works.

Second, the Christian should put things into focus. Recognizing that the Scripture tells man why he is here brings matters into sharp focus. Man has been given authority by God to "subdue the earth" (Genesis 1:26-31). David contemplates God's staggering injunction to have dominion over all the earth in Psalm 8:3-6. Here we find some plain and profound answers to basic human questions. What is man? Man is a creation of God and he is crowned with God's glory and honor. Why is man? That is, what is his purpose? Psalm 8:6 says that God has put man in charge of everything He has made; everything is put under man's authority. (See Psalm 8:6, *Living Psalms*.) When the Christian can sharply focus the tremendous truths of who he is and what his purpose is, he has a solid foundation for moving out into the world and into life to discover God's particular will for him.

Third, the Christian can be scientific by practicing the scientist's code, which is very similar to the Christian ethics taught in Scripture. The virtues of the scientist, that is, those attitudes that make science possible, include truthfulness, honesty, integrity, humility, patience and cooperation. Although science has long since departed from its Christian origins, these virtues are adopted and practiced by scientists the world over to one degree or another.* Certainly the Christian should be able to do the same and do it far better because the Christian has the indwelling power of the Holy Spirit (Romans 8:5) while the unbelieving scientist operates in his own strength.

What is constantly embarrassing to Christians is that many unbelieving scientists seem to practice these virtues and ethics far more successfully and consistently than do those who claim that they know Christ as personal Saviour and Lord. This does not mean that Christ or Christianity lacks power, but it does mean that many Christians lack the faith and trust to put themselves completely in God's hands. Every day can be a day of tremendous adventure and thrilling scientific experiment for the Christian as he opens himself to the guidance and leading of God.

Fourth, the Christian can think God's thoughts after Him and use science to glorify God, not man. The church does not have to fear knowledge and scientific advancement. In fact, the church has every reason to welcome learning because ultimately the truth of science will affirm the truth of Scripture. For the Christian to belittle the contributions of scientific research is to suggest that his faith may not be true after

*See "The Sources of Science," David F. Siemens, Journal of the American Scientific Affiliation, September, 1966, p. 86.

all and that he is afraid science, not God, is the answer to life. If the Christian is convinced that he has the truth, he will want to promote scientific research.*

Potential and opportunity for the scientific Christian is unlimited. Science continues to achieve technologically at a dizzying pace, and at the same time mankind continues to flounder morally at an alarming rate.

Dr. Max Born, co-winner of the Nobel Prize in physics in 1954, is pessimistic about man's ability to survive his own technological development. Born fears that the scientific method, which challenges all absoletes and traditions, has caused a break in civilization that may be irreparable. If the break is irreparable, Born fears it means an end to man as a free, responsible being.

Born says that even if the human race should avoid extinguishing itself by nuclear war, it will still be in danger of degenerating into ". . . a flock of stupid, dumb creatures under the tyranny of dictators who rule them with the help of machines and electronic computers."**

Is there any hope that men can escape the clutches of "Big Brother" and the inhuman existence that some writers predict will occur by 1984?*** Born hopes for a man, "cleverer and wiser" than any before in history, who can lead the world out of its impasse.

Other scientists, quoted in *Christianity Today*,**** believe that Man has already been here:

"Have science and technology solved man's basic problems: the quest for ultimate truth by which to live and to die, the problems of moral and intellectual corruption, of crime, war, and suffering? 'It is evident that mere scientific

*See **Modern Science and the Christian Faith**, John W. Klotz, Concordia Publishing House, 1961, p. 137.
See "Fears of a Scientist," Dr. Max Born, condensed from the **Bulletin of the Atomic Scientists, November, 1965, reprinted in **The Christian Reader**, April-May, 1966.
***See 1984, George Orwell, Harcourt, Brace and Co., Inc., 1949.
****These quotes are from "What Some Scientists Say About God and the Supernatural," **Christianity Today**, August 27, 1965.

knowledge, however valuable, can never accomplish this . . . Rather do I believe in the God of the Bible as a person, and faith in Him to me means commitment to Jesus as the Christ. Actual communication with Him changes man's life from within: it is here that the answer is waiting.' " —Dr. Bodo Volkman, Mathematics Professor.

"Science tells us what we can do, but it cannot tell us what we ought to do. In my own life, ultimate personal questions find their solution in my relationship to God through the person of Jesus Christ." —Dr. Walter R. Hearn, Biochemist.

"Man today is finding that science as such offers no explanation of the facts of human self-consciousness and of the freedom of choice experienced in human personality, which itself is the reason for man's interest in scientific knowledge or indeed in any kind of truth." —Dr. Walter Rollier Thorson, Chemist, Massachusetts Institute of Technology.

If Christians could succeed in re-establishing the concept of seeking knowledge "for the glory of God," they would change the whole intellectual climate of academic circles. Secularism and atheism would cease being the only options available to intellectual minds.* Christians could once again set the pace in man's conquest of ignorance and sin and more directly fulfill God's commission to have dominion over the earth and to show the excellence of God's name in all the earth! Psalm 8:6 says that God has put all things under man's feet. He has dominion over all the earth, but he still must look to and obey his Creator, who is the source of all his accomplishments and of life itself.

*See "Christianity and Science," Kenneth L. Pike, **The Church Herald**, November 26, 1965.

For Further Reading

Paperbacks

Faith and the Physical World: A Comprehensive View, David L. Dye, William B. Eerdmans Publishing Company, 1966. A holder of a Ph.D. in physics who later became chief of the

Radiation Effects Organization at Boeing Airplane Company, Dr. Dye points out the failures in scientism and the need for a world view of life philosophy that includes faith in God. See especially the introduction and chapters 2 and 3 on "Physical Reality," and "Christian Pre-suppositions."

Hardbacks

Protestant Christian Evidences, Bernard Ramm, Moody Press, 1954. A good discussion of anti-supernaturalism versus supernaturalism, which gives the layman a good grounding in basic Christian apologetics.

The Christian View of Science and Scripture, Bernard Ramm, William B. Eerdmans Publishing Company, 1955. See especially chapters 1, 2, and 3 which deal with the "conflict" between theology and science and the fundamental problems of Christianity and science.

So You Want To Be A Scientist?, Allen E. Nourse, Harper and Bros., 1960. The basic information on what it means and what it takes to be a scientist in today's world.

The Universe: Planned or Accident?, Robert E. D. Clark, Muhlenberg Press, 1961. Clark takes issue with a typical criticism of Christianity by the believer in scientism, namely that Christians believe in a "God of the gaps," meaning gaps in their knowledge.

Periodicals

Journalism of the American Scientific Affiliation is a quarterly publication containing the contemporary ideas and thinking from among some 400 members of the American Scientific Affiliation, men of science who are also committed Christians. These Christian geologists, geneticists, biologists, physicists, etc. contribute regularly to the *Journal of the ASA* with articles to interpret the findings of science according to God's revealed truth in Scripture. *The ASA Journal* is available quarterly from: Executive Secretary, the American Scientific Affiliation, 324½ South Second Street, Mankato, Minnesota, 56001. Cost, $5.00 per year.

"What Some Scientists Say About God and the Supernatural," *Christianity Today*, August 27, 1965, p. 5-13. An outstanding symposium quoting some three dozen scientists concerning their belief in God and the Christ of the Bible.

"Does the Bible Conflict with Modern Science?" *Christianity Today*, January 21, 1966, p. 3-6. A panel discussion between three distinguished scientists and Carl F. H. Henry, editor of *Christianity Today*. Included among the scientists who proclaim their Christian beliefs are Dr. Martin J. Buerger, world renowned expert in crystallography and mineralogy and professor at Massachusetts Institute of Technology; Dr. Charles Hatfield, Chairman of the Department of Mathematics at the University of Missouri; Dr. William G. Pollard, Executive Director of the Oakridge Institute of Nuclear Studies, who in 1954 was ordained to the Episcopal priesthood.

"Must We Be Afraid of Science?" Laurence Kulp, *Eternity*, May, 1963, p. 17. Excellent advice on how to be a "scientific" Christian in the space age. An outstanding geologist, Dr. Kulp shows that science is not a "devil" to be fought or feared but a friend to be used for the glory of God.

"Science versus Theology: The Battle Isn't Over Yet," Bernard Ramm, *Eternity*, October 1965, p. 17. Theologian Ramm traces the history of the battle between science and theology over the centuries and focuses on the struggle involving the conflict of evolutionism and Scripture. His article is adapted from a paper released earlier in the *ASA Journal*. See also in the same October 1965 issue of *Eternity*, "Public Schools, Science, and your Children" by V. Elving Anderson and "Let's Be Honest About Evolution," James Hefley.

"Is Christianity Rational?" Paul E. Little, *Moody Monthly*, September 1967, p. 36. The Director for Evangelism, Inter-Varsity Christian Fellowship, Mr. Little writes with clarity and common sense on the meaning of Christian faith in a secular and scientific world. He includes this quote by John Stott: "We cannot pander to a man's intellectual arrogance, but we must cater to his intellectual integrity." This article is adapted from a chapter in Mr. Little's book, *Know Why You Believe*, Scripture Press, 1967.

CONCLUSION

Can straw men keep you from God?

At first glance (or first reading) this book might seem to some to be another attempt to "defend the orthodox establishment." *Who Says?* has a pugnacious sound, which sort of reminds you of "Do you wanna fight?"

In a way, this book does want to fight, but not with real people (who are entitled to their opinions and who are free to form these opinions as they will). *Who Says?* has a quarrel, rather, with the "straw men" that keep real men and women from making their own rational choice about Jesus Christ and a personal relationship to God.

Granted, there has been "defense of orthodoxy" in the preceding pages, but the goal is not simply protection of tradition for tradition's sake. The goal is a clear presentation of the basic issues behind such questions as "Who says the Bible is truth, not myth?" or "Who says that today's secular man (who has come of scientific age) needs God anyway?"

The goal of *Who Says?* is to get you to analyze the basic philosophies and points of view behind certain criticisms of Christianity, the Bible, the church, and believers in general. Not that Christians are not open to criticism. They fall woefully short of the life their Master calls them to live. But behind many anti-Christian criticisms, the "straw men" lie in wait, ready to ambush rational thought and a fair examination of all the evidence. (And ironically, a lot of this assassination of rational and reasonable thinking is done in the name of rationalism.)

Dr. William R. Bright puts it this way . . .

"Have you ever seriously analyzed what it is that is keeping you from God? Why you don't know Him personally? Many who now know Him once rejected what they thought was Christianity. Arnold Toynbee, the eminent historian, said, "Most people have not rejected Christianity. They have rejected a caricature." They have actually created a straw man, called it Christianity, and decided against it.

"Famous skeptics such as Paine, Voltaire, and Ingersoll have gone to great ends to justify their rejection of Christianity. However, a careful study of their reasons shows that what has been rejected as Christianity is but a straw man fabricated out of erroneous concepts and misunderstandings.

"Some people who reject Christianity give as their reason an unhappy experience with a childhood Sunday School teacher. Others see the hypocrisy of some professing Christians. Others judge Christianity by corruption in the church during history.

"Too often, Christianity is viewed as just a way of life

—involving church attendance, giving offerings, and trying to live by the golden rule.

"What does Christianity mean to you? Does the word suggest steeples, prayers, sermons, and the Ten Commandments? Do you think of a story you heard about some religious leader or an unpleasant experience with a professing Christian? Are these your straw men? Genuine paper currency always seems to have its counterfeit. Would it be rational to reject the genuine because the counterfeit also exists?

"The universe shows design. It would be ridiculous to conclude that man is without purpose, even more to conclude that God has not revealed this purpose to man. God's plan and love are explained in the Bible and fully revealed in the person of Jesus Christ. Yet many have attended church for years, struggled to reform, tried to live by the golden rule, then fell back in utter frustration. Inevitable discouragement and disillusionment set in when they failed to find, through religious activity, the reality they were seeking.

"Quite often a negative attitude followed. Doubts filled their minds. Finally, what these people thought was Christianity was rejected. The straw man had been set up and knocked over.

"Could this be you? Are you among those who honestly want to know God? A simple plan will help. First, read the Gospel of John in the New Testament with a receptive spirit. Second, carefully explain who Jesus Christ is and why He came to earth. Third, define a Christian. Fourth, write down the best reasons you can think of for not becoming a Christian. Are you sure that what you are rejecting is true Christianity?

"Now consider a living Person, Jesus Christ, not a religion, a particular church, minister, or Christian. Simply consider Christ: His sinless life, His claims to be the Son of God, His resurrection from the dead, and

His vast influence for good through the centuries. What do you find wrong with Him?

"True Christianity is Christ living His life in and through an individual. Carefully read the following Scripture portions: Gospel of John 3:1-8; Ephesians 2:8,9; First Epistle of John 5:11-15; Revelation 3:20; Gospel of John 1:12. Christ can forgive and cleanse you of your sin and fill your heart with a peace that cannot be experienced in any other way. Simply confess your need and invite Him to make Himself known to you as Saviour and Lord."*

Does Dr. Bright's advice sound too simple—too much like the "invitation" at the close of the service, the sawdust trail down which the "orthodox establishment" wants everyone to walk to make sure they are "saved"?

Careful . . . this stereotype of the gospel can be a "straw man" too. We live in a secular society—a society that is jaded and cynical—suspicious of being "taken in," especially by religion.

But who says Dr. Bright is merely talking about "religion"? Is the issue really religion *or is it God himself?*

What follows is an item from the magazine *Christianity Today* (August 18, 1967). The writer is Dr. James W. Didier, University Baptist Chaplain, Michigan State University. Entitled "Secular Man?", it is a sort of parable—an earthly story of "secular everyman" and the need for heavenly meaning in his life. Here is the account. It concludes *Who Says?* There is much more that can be written on Christian apologetics, but there is really not anything else to say. . .

* * * *

*"Are Straw Men Keeping You From God?" William R. Bright, Collegiate Challenge, Campus Crusade for Christ, Arrowhead Springs, San Bernardino, California.

He had been away from college for several years and had now come to the university to work on a Ph.D. in one of the social sciences. His hometown pastor had written me a brief note suggesting I call on him.

We arranged to have lunch in the cafeteria of his university residence hall. He greeted me amicably, and we went through the lunch line. We sat at a small corner table and proceeded almost directly to the matter at hand.

He related his early experience with the church. Typical. His mother had taught Sunday school for years. He was baptized as a young adolescent and held local and regional youth leadership positions. His undergraduate years were spent in the custodial care of an evangelical college. Then five years in the business world. A gradual drift away from religion. Now, no concern for the church. For several years he had been rather hostile toward Christianity; now he was just neutral.

He was matter-of-fact in saying he had outgrown the need for religion. He stated with some feeling, "I could never go back to what I had. No satisfaction. No freedom." He went on, "Perhaps some day, when I'm about forty, I might work out a religious frame of reference, but I doubt it will ever happen. Right now I'm too busy sucking all of life in. There's just too much to experience, and I'm hungry for a full life."

As we rose from the table, I noticed that he had tasted each food but had finished only the cake. As we walked back to his room, he told me he had concluded that there was no synthesis for life. He had discovered that all that matters is that we play effectively our chosen role and do whatever is at hand with professional competence.

Back in his room I mentioned that I had not detected in his words any hint of his purpose for undertaking graduate study. I asked whether his decision was based partly on a desire to do something for others or make the world a bit better. He hadn't any such idea, he said. He readily acknowledged that his life was self-centered and said he didn't believe persons who say they are trying to invest their lives for the sake of others or for the sake of God. "They are hypocrites. All that matters is that we do our job well." And, "Man is his own measure of all things."

"Religion," he reaffirmed, "is no longer personally relevant. It simply has no bearing on my life, nor, for that matter, on the lives of most people I know." Then after a reflective pause: "To be honest, I would have to say that rather than having actually outgrown the claims of Christ, I believe I make a more or less deliberate effort to ignore them."

An awkward silence.

I suggested that we try to keep in touch and stood up as though to leave.

We shook hands.

I noticed that his hand was wet with perspiration. He noticed it, too, and quickly withdrew his hand. His eyes opened wide and his jaw dropped a bit. With a tone of surprise he blurted, "My God, my hands are wet."

Silence.

"Yes, I noticed."